How to Train Your

Bichon Frise

liz palika

BICHON
FRISE

Photos by the author unless
otherwise credited.

The Publisher would like to thank the owners of dogs pictured in this book, including: Gail Antetomaso, Halima Blanton, Karen Chesbro, Michael Coad, Kerry Diekman, Toby Frisch, Eleanor Grassick, J. Hilmer, The Hubers, Emil Kauranen, Estelle and Wendy Kellerman, Robert Koepell, Michelle and Karen Konik, David Melberg, The Nolans, Jerome Podell, Rico Ronquillo, Claire Schlegel, Stephen Wojculewski

© T.F.H. Publications, Inc.

Distributed in the UNITED STATES to the Pet Trade by T.F.H. Publications, Inc., 1 TFH Plaza, Neptune City, NJ 07753; on the Internet at www.tfh.com; in CANADA by Rolf C. Hagen Inc., 3225 Sartelon St., Montreal, Quebec H4R 1E8; Pet Trade by H & L Pet Supplies Inc., 27 Kingston Crescent, Kitchener, Ontario N2B 2T6; in ENGLAND by T.F.H. Publications, PO Box 74, Havant PO9 5TT; in AUSTRALIA AND THE SOUTH PACIFIC by T.F.H. (Australia), Pty. Ltd., Box 149, Brookvale 2100 N.S.W., Australia; in NEW ZEALAND by Brooklands Aquarium Ltd., 5 McGiven Drive, New Plymouth, RD1 New Zealand; in SOUTH AFRICA by Rolf C. Hagen S.A. (PTY.) LTD., P.O. Box 201199, Durban North 4016, South Africa; in JAPAN by T.F.H. Publications, Japan—Jiro Tsuda, 10-12-3 Ohjidai, Sakura, Chiba 285, Japan. Published by T.F.H. Publications, Inc.

MANUFACTURED IN THE
UNITED STATES OF AMERICA
BY T.F.H. PUBLICATIONS, INC.

contents

INTRODUCTION

Buttons is a Bichon Frise owned by Claire Schlegel of Escondido, California. This ten-month-old, white, fluffy bundle of joy is training to become a therapy dog. He and his owner recently completed their required obedience training and are now learning the skills necessary to visit people in hospitals, nursing homes, and other facilities where Buttons can share his warmth, love, and affection with the people who need it most.

Right now Buttons is young and still very enthusiastic. He would prefer to cover everyone's face with kisses, wagging his tail as he does. Although kisses are often welcome, he also must learn self-control—waiting to be invited to give kisses, for example—and that's very hard for him. His owner says, "Sitting or standing still while someone pets Buttons is very difficult for him. But he's learning!"

Buttons is a very nice example of a Bichon Frise. He is handsome, intelligent, and has a wonderful white coat that his owner works very hard to keep looking nice. He has been well socialized as a puppy, which is very important for a future therapy dog, and is very good with people and other dogs. He is very affectionate, as are most Bichons.

However, Button's owner isn't the first Bichon owner to

The Bichon Frise is a small, compact, white "powder puff" of a dog with a merry temperament and a dark-eyed inquisitive expression.

bichon frise

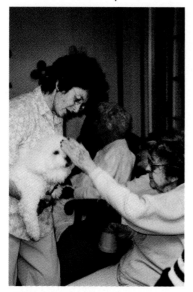

The Bichon's attractive appearance, playful personality, and affectionate nature make him a wonderful companion for people of all ages. This is "Buttons" and his owner, Claire Schlegal, working toward therapy dog certification.

For this book, I talked to many owners of Bichons who have attended my obedience training classes and to the owners of Bichons who are members of the Foundation for Pet Provided Therapy. I asked them how their dogs responded to training, what problems they faced before and during training, and what seemed to work best while training their dogs. We talked about the breed's characteristics and reactions to training.

Prospective owners of Bichons need to know what to expect of the breed—preferably *before* they get a new dog—and Bichon owners need to know what makes this breed tick. Although Bichons are wonderful dogs, they are not the right breed for everyone. I would prefer that people figure that out before they get a Bichon rather than discover it later after the dog is already a part of the family.

admit the breed is not perfect. As with all breeds of dog, the Bichon has some characteristics that can make life interesting (to say the least!). She says, "Buttons is very active and would prefer to play a lot—a lot more than I can reasonably play with him! He is easily excited and sometimes it takes a while to calm him down. When he gets excited, he barks, and I have to work with him to keep that barking under control so that it doesn't become annoying."

In this book, I have tried to present Bichon Frise owners (and prospective owners) with information about choosing a dog and how to make that dog a well-behaved member of the family. With training and help from their owners, Bichons can be fun-loving, energetic clowns as well as affectionate, loving companions.

SELECTING
the Right Dog for You

WHAT ARE BICHONS?

In the Beginning

The early Romans were great fans of dogs and had devised a system of classifying dogs as early as the first century AD. Dogs were sorted into categories such as home guardian dogs, livestock guardian dogs, herding dogs, scent hunting dogs, sight hunting dogs, and war dogs. The Romans developed breeds of dog on their own or by confiscating dogs they admired in the countries they conquered. Various breeds were developed by breeding dogs with similar characteristics— either working abilities or physical similarities—together. Sometimes an entirely new type of dog would be created by breeding different dogs together.

A number of different varieties of dog were used to create a family of similar dogs called the "barbichons." This was later shortened to "bichon." These small, light-

Originating in the Mediterranean region centuries ago, Bichons have a long history as companion dogs. Their small size, delicate beauty, and charm made the breed a fashionable pet and a favorite of royalty.

Photo by Robert Pearcy

bichon frise

colored dogs were very popular family dogs. During their travels through Europe, these dogs became popular in other places, too, and eventually, four varieties were identified. The Bichon Maltaise is thought to have been the ancestor of today's Maltese. The Bichon Havanais (Havanese) is similar to today's Bichon Frise except that it is shorter in height, has a longer body and shorter legs than the Frise, and is found in other colors than white. The Bichon Bolognaise was very popular in Italy and is very similar to today's Bichon Frise.

Photo by Isabelle Francais

During the 19th century, Europe's great circuses and carnivals took advantage of the Bichon's uncanny ability to learn and perform tricks. Highly trainable, they have the unique ability to walk on their hind legs for long distances, a trait still seen today.

CROWD PLEASERS

In the 1500s, France invaded Italy many times. As with all occupational forces, the invading army was influenced by the culture of the area. History records that Bichons began appearing in France during the 1500s, probably brought home by soldiers who had invaded and occupied Italy. In France, these agile, intelligent, and acrobatic little dogs quickly became favorites of street musicians, organ grinders, and traders. The dogs could perform tricks, dance, and otherwise attract the crowd's attention. Their ability to walk on their hind legs and wave their front paws in the air is still seen in today's Bichons.

The Bichon Tenerife is thought to be the ancestor of today's Bichon Frise. Richard Beauchamp, a well-known dog show exhibitor, author, and judge, was instrumental in achieving American Kennel Club (AKC) recognition for the Bichon Frise. He says of the breed's history, "The Bichon seems to have flourished in the Canary Islands and Tenerife as well. Eventually their descendants made their way full circle, back to Spain and Italy. This variety of Bichon was known as the Bichon Tenerife, and the breed was to carry that name for many years."

The Bichon Frise Today

The Bichon Frise was recognized by the American Kennel Club in 1973 as a Non-Sporting breed. The Bichon is a small dog, between 9 and 11 inches tall. He has a compact body, with the length of the body just slightly longer than the dog is tall. A Bichon should appear sturdy without appearing coarse or heavy.

COAT CARE

Potential Bichon owners should remember that this coat requires a great deal of care to keep it healthy and looking nice. Daily grooming is a necessity—at least half an hour per day to thoroughly brush and comb the coat. Without daily care, this coat can easily tangle and mat. Burrs and foxtails can create havoc in the coat, causing tangles and mats that may have to be trimmed out. Fleas and ticks are also disasters, especially if the dog starts to chew on himself. Bichon owners must set aside regular time each day to care for the dog's coat.

The Bichon's plush white coat is his trademark. Potential owners should realize that it will require considerable daily grooming to keep it healthy and looking nice.

Photo by Isabelle Francais

bichon frise

Nor should he appear fine or fragile.

A big part of the Bichon's appeal is his wonderful expression. The eyes are dark, large, and should convey the breed's alertness, inquisitive nature, and sense of fun. Even though the breed is white, there should be dark skin around the eyes. The nose is also black, as are the lips.

The Bichon's lovely white coat is his trademark. The coat is always white, although there may be some minor shadings of cream, buff, or apricot around the ears. The undercoat is soft and dense, while the outercoat is slightly more curly and has a coarser texture than the undercoat. When freshly bathed and brushed, the coat will stand out like a substantial powder-puff. When not freshly brushed, the coat will be closer to the body and will show more curl.

Temperament

Bichon Frises are, more than anything else, happy dogs. Whereas some breeds are very serious (Rottweilers, for example) and some breeds are very tenacious (like Welsh Terriers), Bichons are merry, happy, and fun-loving. This breed is also very affectionate and can be extremely demanding when it wants attention from its owner.

Benjamin L. Hart, DVM, and Lynette A. Hart, authors of *The Perfect Puppy,* which ranked many of the more popular breeds according to certain characteristics, listed the Bichon Frise as easy to housetrain, willing to accept obedience training, and very affectionate. The Harts also ranked the Bichon as very playful. A trait that goes along with playfulness is a tendency toward destructive behavior. The Bichon may chew on things that he shouldn't chew on, so this needs to be taken into consideration during training. Luckily, the small size of the

Your local pet shop sells excellent grooming supplies, which can sometimes be purchased in affordable combination packages. Photo courtesy of Wahl, USA.

reactive to the world around them. Because the Bichon is reactive but not at all aggressive, he may bark when someone approaches the house, but everyone entering will be more likely to be greeted with kisses than with growls.

As a general rule, Bichon Frises are happy, fun-loving dogs with a merry twinkle in their eye. They are active, playful, and sometimes destructive, but are also intelligent and easily trained. Bichons are affectionate and will demand to be with their owner as much as possible.

Playful and fun-loving, Bichons are also very affectionate and can be extremely demanding when they want attention from their owners.

Photo by Isabelle Francais

Bichon can limit the amount of damage the dog can do.

Bichons are also very active dogs and can be very reactive to the world around them. This reactivity means the dogs pay attention to things—someone walking down the street will gain their attention, whereas many other breeds would ignore the person unless he or she came up the walk to the door.

The Bichon should not be considered a watchdog or guard dog even though they are very

IS A BICHON FRISE THE RIGHT DOG FOR YOU?

Evaluating Your Personality and Lifestyle

The decision to add a dog to your family is not one to be taken lightly. This is a 14- to 15-year commitment, and Bichons are intelligent, affectionate dogs with some specific needs.

Do you work long hours, come home tired, and just want to relax by spending the evening reading or watching television? If you do, an older, more mature Bichon Frise would be a better choice for you than a puppy or young dog. Do you come home tired but enjoy doing things outside, such as gardening or going for a walk? If so, an adult dog might be suited to your lifestyle. Do you work at home, have short work hours, and enjoy doing things? If so, a puppy or an active young dog should please you.

Being the center of a dog's world can be thrilling to some people and overwhelming to others. If you don't like being followed, watched, or touched, don't get a Bichon Frise. A Bichon will want to be close to you and follow you from room to room. When you sit down, your Bichon will be next to you on the sofa, on your lap, or

Because Bichons are social dogs that bond strongly with everyone in the family, your companionship is necessary to their happiness and well-being.

Dog ownership is a long-term commitment; so be sure your lifestyle will permit you to fulfill your Bichon's needs for vigorous exercise, training, and daily companionship. If you don't appreciate a dog's closeness—don't get a Bichon!

Photo by Isabelle Francais

bichon frise

Photo by Robert Pearcy

Bichons are a very intelligent and outgoing breed, and if you don't train your Bichon, he'll train you!

lying at your feet. When you leave the house, the Bichon will want to go with you. Obviously, having a dog with you for 24 hours a day is impossible for most people. However, if you want a Bichon Frise, you will need to be able to provide as much companionship as possible.

Before thinking of getting a Bichon Frise, look at your life as realistically as possible. A Bichon could be a wonderful companion for many people but is not the right breed for all people. A Bichon should not be left alone for many hours a day.

Also, a Bichon should not be owned by a person who doesn't appreciate a dog's closeness or by someone who doesn't enjoy activity.

The Bichon Frise's Needs

All dogs have some specific needs that you must think about before you add a dog to your family. It could mean the difference between a successful relationship with a dog or the need to give the dog up later.

First of all, your companionship is very important. As was mentioned earlier, Bichons need to spend time with their people. You must also be willing to take the time to train your Bichon Frise. Bichons are very intelligent, and if you don't train your Bichon Frise, he will train you!

You will need to have a securely fenced yard or dog run. As a curious, social dog, Bichons left alone may try to escape from the yard to find human companionship or to look for you. A large, securely fenced yard is wonderful, but even a dog run (no smaller than 6 feet by 20 feet) is acceptable as long as the dog gets plenty of time out of the run when you're at home.

You must also have some means of exercising your Bichon

Frise. A vigorous walk is fine for a young Bichon or an older dog, but a healthy adult Bichon will need more strenuous daily exercise. If you like to go jogging, that's fine, but if you are not a jogger you will need to think of some other way of exercising your dog. Teach your Bichon to chase and bring back a tennis ball or Frisbee™—that's good exercise.

SELECTING THE RIGHT DOG

Male or Female?

There are a lot of myths about the personality traits of both males and females. Ultimately, it depends on the personality of the individual dog. Spayed bitches (females) and neutered dogs (males) are usually a little calmer. Spaying and neutering removes the sexual hormones and, as a result, the sexual tension that can accompany those hormones. To be a good pet and companion, your Bichon Frise doesn't need those hormones anyway.

Male Bichons tend to be a little more territorial than females, and females tend to accept training better than males. However, both of these statements are generalizations, and individual dogs (and bitches) may vary from these tendencies.

What Age?

Puppies are adorable, especially Bichon Frise puppies

A highly athletic and curious breed, the Bichon will need some form of strenuous daily exercise or else he may find less constructive ways to release his energy.

bichon frise

13

An adult dog may be just the answer for people who do not have the patience or time to spend housebreaking and training a puppy.

with their round tummies, big heads, and fluffy puppy coats. However, when you add a puppy to your family, it's just like adding a baby to the family. Puppies, just like babies, need to eat often, sleep a lot, and relieve themselves often. In short, they demand a lot of your time.

As your puppy grows, he will become an integral part of your family. By the time your Bichon Frise is grown up (in two years), your dog will have become a good friend. In the meantime, raising a puppy is a lot of work. For many people, a puppy is not an option. But that doesn't mean these people can't have a dog. There are many adult Bichons that need good homes, and one of these dogs could be just the thing for people who do not have the time or patience to deal with a young puppy.

There are some drawbacks to adopting an adult dog. The process can be compared to buying a used car—sometimes you get a gem and sometimes you get a lemon. You don't know how the dog has been treated prior to your ownership, and that can affect future behavior. Many times, too, the dog's health history is unknown.

Newly adopted dogs must also have time to adjust to their

new homes emotionally and physically. Because Bichons are so attached to their people, changing homes can be very traumatic. A newly adopted Bichon Frise may be very clingy, showing signs of separation anxiety whenever he is left alone. Usually these behaviors will decrease as the dog settles into the new home, bonds with his new owners, and feels more comfortable.

Finding an Adult Dog

If you have decided that an adult Bichon Frise would be better for you than a puppy, there are a few different places where you can look for your new companion. Check your local shelter or humane society. Bichons are given up for a variety of reasons: Perhaps the owner passed away, was transferred overseas, or didn't realize what a Bichon Frise was like and gave him up after a few months. What ever the reason, when people give up their dog, they often bring him to the local shelter.

Evaluating an Adult Dog

Once you have found an adult Bichon Frise, how do you

Before deciding to bring a Bichon puppy into your home, it is important to do your homework and learn as much as you can about the breed.

Photo by Isabelle Francais

bichon frise

decide whether he is the right dog for you? First of all, do you like this dog? Your feelings for the dog are certainly going to play a big part in your relationship, and if you don't feel something right away, you should probably keep looking. However, don't say yes to this dog just because you like him. There is more to this decision than that.

Do you know why this dog was given up by his owner? Sometimes the dog is given up through no fault of his own. However, if the owner gave up the dog because of behavior problems, you need to know that. Has the dog had any obedience training? Is the dog

RESCUE GROUPS

Many breed clubs sponsor or run breed rescue groups. Rescue groups screen the dogs they take in for adoption, and this can be very beneficial to you. The dogs will have been checked by an expert in the breed for personality flaws (such as aggressiveness) and for their obedience skills (or lack thereof). The dogs are vaccinated, spayed, or neutered. This screening process can take some of the uncertainty out of the adoption process. To find a Bichon Frise rescue group in your area, check with your local shelter or humane society.

housetrained? These are important issues, because even if you are willing to do some

There are many places you can look for a canine companion—check with your local shelter or humane society.

Photo by Vince Serbin

bichon frise

training, housetraining a previously untrained adult Bichon Frise can be quite an undertaking.

What is the dog's personality like? Bichons are usually happy dogs, with a touch of the clown visible in their eyes and smile. However, a great many things can affect a dog's personality, including poor breeding practices, a lack of socialization as a puppy, and more. When you whistle or speak to the dog, what does he do? Does he look at you and wag his tail? Great! If he looks sideways at you, slinks, or bares his throat, be careful. This dog is worried

Photo by Isabelle Francais

Attending a dog show in your area is a good way to get information and breeder referrals from Bichon experts and owners.

To help ensure a successful relationship with your Bichon, choose a dog whose personality will suit yours. For example, an active, playful dog is a good match for an outgoing extrovert, whereas a quiet, submissive dog would do well with a quiet person or less active retiree.

or scared, and a fearful dog can bite. Be careful, too, if the dog stands on his tiptoes and stares you in the eye. This is a challenging dog and could be potentially aggressive. Even a small dog can hurt you or your children if he bites.

Ideally, you want a dog that is happy to see you without showing too much worry or fearfulness and without showing any aggression. You want a dog that is housetrained and has hopefully had some basic training. Make sure the dog's behavior problems are ones that you can live with for the time being and are willing to work on in the future.

Photo by Robert Pearcy

Responsible breeders ensure that good health and temperament are passed down to each succeeding generation.

Finding a Puppy

If you have the time, patience, and resources to raise a puppy, you will want to find a reputable breeder. Breeder referrals can come from many sources. People walking their dogs can refer you to their breeder. Your veterinarian might have a Bichon Frise breeder as a client. Many of the national dog magazines have advertisements for breeders. You may also want to attend a dog show in your community and talk to people there.

Once you find a few breeders, make an appointment to meet with them. At this meeting, ask the breeder a few questions: "Are you active in dog shows and dog sports?" If the breeders show their dogs in conformation dog shows, their dogs are probably good examples of the breed. If they participate in obedience competitions, their dogs are trainable.

"Do you belong to the national and local Bichon Frise clubs?" Breeders who do are more likely to be up-to-date on news within the breed. Breed club newsletters and magazines usually publish articles on the breed's health and well-being.

"What health problems have you seen in your dogs?" If the breeder says none, be skeptical. A breed or line with no health problems at all is rare. Bichons can have a number of problems, including allergies. The breeders should be honest with you about potential health threats and what they are doing to try to prevent future problems.

"Can you provide me with a list of references?" Of course, the breeder will give you a list of people she knows are happy with her dogs, but that's okay. You can still ask people about their experience: "Did the breeder work well with you?" "Did she provide all the promised paperwork?" "Would you buy a puppy from her again?"

Caring breeders will ask you as many questions as you ask them. They want to know if you are the right person for one of their puppies. Don't get defensive—they are trying to do the right thing. Instead, answer the questions honestly. If by some chance, a breeder says her dogs are not right for you, listen to her. She knows her dogs better than you do.

Evaluating a Puppy

Each puppy has his own personality and finding the right personality to match yours is sometimes a challenge. For example, if you are outgoing, extroverted, and active, a quiet, withdrawn, submissive puppy would not fit well into your household and lifestyle. You will need a puppy more like you. On the other hand, that quiet puppy might do very well with a shy person or a less active retiree.

When you go look at a litter of puppies, there are a few things you can do with each puppy to help evaluate his personality. First, take the puppy away from his mother or littermates. Place the puppy on the ground and walk a few steps away from him. Squat down and call the puppy to you. An outgoing, extroverted puppy will come happily and try to climb in your lap. If you stand up and walk away, the extrovert will follow you, trying to get underfoot. If you throw a piece of crumpled paper a few feet away, he will dash after it quickly. This Bichon Frise would do well with an owner who is just as much of an extrovert as he is. He will need training to

The Bichon puppy you choose should be bright eyed, healthy, responsive, and curious about the world around him.

Photo by Isabelle Francais

Watching the way a Bichon puppy behaves with his littermates will tell you a lot about his personality.

teach him self-control, lots of exercise, and a job to occupy his bright mind.

A quiet, submissive puppy will come to you when you call but may do a belly crawl or roll over and bare his belly. When you get up to walk away, he will watch you but may be hesitant to follow you. If you toss the paper, he may go after it but may be hesitant to bring it back to you. This puppy will need a quiet owner, gentle handling, and positive training.

These two puppies are the extremes for Bichon Frise temperaments, and most Bichons are somewhere in between these two personality types. Try to find a puppy with a personality that will be comfortable for you. Don't get an active puppy in the hopes of becoming more active yourself if you are sedentary by nature. It won't work, and the active puppy will drive you nuts! Nor should you get a puppy with a certain personality in hopes of changing him—that won't work either. Find the puppy that is right for you.

BE CAREFUL!

Adding a Bichon Frise to your family should be a time of anticipation and excitement, but making it work requires thought, research, and preparation. Without preparation, the entire process could easily become a nightmare. Unfortunately, horror stories abound of puppies bought or adopted on impulse and given up later because the relationship didn't work. A Bichon will be a friend and companion for the next 14 years, so first make sure this is the right breed for you and choose the right dog carefully

Canine
DEVELOPMENT
Canine
Stages
2

UNDERSTANDING THE DOG-OWNER BOND

Experts now believe that dogs were first domesticated as much as 135,000 years ago. In spite of this long, shared history, the bond that we have with dogs must be renewed with each puppy. The bond itself is not hereditary, although the tendency to bond is. This relationship is what makes owning a dog so special, but it doesn't happen automatically. To understand when and how this bond develops, it's important to understand that your Bichon is a dog, not a person in a fuzzy dog suit.

Families and Packs

Most researchers agree that the ancestors of today's dogs were wolves. They disagree on what wolves those ancestors were—either the ancestors of today's gray wolves or perhaps a species of wolf that is now extinct. In any event, wolves are social creatures that live in an extended family pack. The pack might consist of a dominant

Like their ancestors the wolves, dogs are social creatures that live in an extended family pack. It is important to establish yourself as the pack leader from the beginning of your relationship with your Bichon.

bichon frise

 The bond of trust and affection that you form with your Bichon when he's a puppy will be helpful later when you begin to train him.

Photo by Isabelle Francais

(alpha) male and a dominant (alpha) female, and these two are usually the only ones that breed. There will also be subordinate males and females, juveniles, and puppies. A wolf pack is a very harmonious group that hunts together, plays together, defends its territory against intruders, and cares for each other. The only discord occurs when there is a change in the pack order. If one of the leaders becomes disabled, an adult leaves the pack, or a subordinate adult tries to assume dominance, there may be some jockeying around to fill that position.

Many experts believe that domesticated dogs adapt so well to our lifestyle because we

For the first few weeks of life, a Bichon puppy's mother is his key to survival and his source of food, warmth, and security.

Photo by Isabelle Francais

also live in groups. We call our groups families instead of packs, but they are still social groups. However, the comparison isn't really accurate—our families are much more chaotic than the average wolf pack. We are terribly inconsistent with our social rules and rules for behavior. (We let our Bichon jump up on the sofa most of the time, but yell at him when he jumps up on the sofa with muddy paws!) To the dog, our communication skills are also confusing. Our voice says one thing while our body language says something else. To our dogs, we are very complex, confusing creatures. While we can say that both dogs and humans live in social groups and use that comparison to understand a little more about our dogs, we must also understand that our families are very different from a wolf pack.

FROM BIRTH TO FOUR WEEKS OF AGE

For the first three weeks of life, the family and the pack are unimportant as far as the baby Bichon is concerned. The only one of any significance is his mother. She is the key to his survival and the source of food, warmth, and security.

A Bichon puppy should never be taken from his mother too soon—the discipline he receives from her during early stages of development will teach the pup to accept correction, training, and affection as he grows into adulthood.

Photo by Isabelle Francais

LET THE MOTHER DOG CORRECT

Some inexperienced breeders will stop the mother dog from correcting her puppies, perhaps thinking that the mother dog is impatient, tired, or a poor mother. When the mother dog is not allowed to correct the puppies naturally, the puppies do not learn how to accept discipline and therefore have a hard time later when their new owner tries to establish some rules. Orphaned puppies raised by people suffer from the same problems. The mother dog knows instinctively what to do for her babies, and sometimes a correction—a low growl, a bark, or a snap of the teeth—is exactly what is needed.

The puppies should never be taken from their mother at this stage of development. Puppies taken away now and sent to new homes may have lasting behavior problems. They often have difficulty dealing with other dogs, may have trouble accepting rules and discipline, and may become excessively shy, aggressive, or fearful.

At four weeks of age, the baby Bichon's needs are still being met by his mother, but his littermates are becoming more important. His brothers and sisters provide warmth and security when their mother leaves the nest. His curiosity is developing, and he will climb on and over his littermates, learning their scent and feel. During this period, he will learn to use his sense of hearing to follow sounds and his sense of vision to follow moving objects.

His mom will also start disciplining the puppies—very gently, of course—and this early discipline is vitally important to the puppies' future acceptance of discipline and training.

The breeder should be handling the puppies now to get them used to gentle handling by people. At this age, the puppies can learn the difference between their mother's touch and a human touch.

WEEKS FIVE THROUGH SEVEN

The young Bichon goes through some tremendous changes between five and seven weeks of age. He is learning to recognize people and is starting to respond to individual voices. He is playing more with his littermates, and the wrestling and scuffling teaches each puppy how to get along, how to play, when the play is too rough, when to be submissive, and what to take seriously. His mother's discipline at this stage of development teaches the puppy to accept corrections, training, and affection.

THE EIGHTH WEEK

The eighth week of life is a frightening time for most puppies. Puppies go through several fear periods during their maturation, and this is the first one. Even though this is the traditional time for most puppies to go to their new homes, they would actually benefit by staying with their littermates for one more week. If the puppy leaves the breeder's home during this fear period and is frightened by the car ride home, he may retain that fear of car rides for the rest of his life. In fact, this stress is why so many puppies get car sick.

The same applies to the puppy's new home, his first trip to the veterinarian's office, or anything else that frightens him.

WEEKS NINE THROUGH TWELVE

The baby Bichon can go to his new home anytime during the ninth and tenth weeks of life. At this age, he is ready to form permanent relationships. Take advantage of this and spend time with your new puppy, playing with him and

Photo by Isabelle Francais

Once separated from his mother and littermates, your Bichon puppy will depend on you to fulfill all his needs. Care, kindness, and encouragement will help ensure that he becomes a well-adjusted pet.

encouraging him to explore his new world. Teach him his name by calling him in a happy, high-pitched voice. Encourage him to follow you by backing away from him, patting your leg, and calling his name.

Socialization is very important now, too. Socialization is more than simply introducing your puppy to other people, dogs, noises, and sounds. It is making sure he is not frightened by these things as you introduce them. For example, once your baby Bichon has had his vaccinations (check with your veterinarian), take your puppy with you to the pet store when you go to buy dog food. While there, introduce your puppy to the store clerks, other customers, and even to the store parrot. Your trip there could also include walking up some stairs, walking on slippery floors, and going through an automatic door. All of these things, introduced gradually and with encouragement and repeated all over town (on different days, of course) add up to a confident, well-socialized puppy.

During this stage of development, your Bichon puppy's pack instincts are developing. He is beginning to understand which people belong to his pack (or family) and which do not. Bichons are not overly protective. In fact, your social puppy may want to give everyone kisses, and that's fine. Let him be social. However, if he does growl at people who do not belong to his family pack, let him know that his behavior is not appropriate.

You can show him his position in the family in several different ways, but one of the easiest is to lay him down, roll him over, and give him a tummy rub. This exercise may seem very simple, but by baring his tummy he is assuming a submissive position to you.

A baby Bichon can go to his new home anytime during the ninth and tenth weeks of life.

Photo by Isabelle Francais

As soon as your Bichon is old enough, take him with you wherever you go. Introducing him to new people, places, and experiences will ensure that your puppy is confident and well socialized.

When his mother corrected him by growling or barking at him, he would roll over and bare his tummy to her, in essence telling her, "Okay! I understand, you're the boss!" When you have him roll over for a tummy rub, you are helping him understand the same message, but you are doing it in a very gentle, loving way.

During this stage of development, discipline is very important. Love, affection, and security are still important, too, of course, but right now your Bichon puppy needs to learn that his life is governed by some rules. Don't allow him to do anything now that you won't want him to continue doing later as a full-grown dog.

WEEKS THIRTEEN THROUGH SIXTEEN

From 13 through 16 weeks of age, your Bichon puppy will be trying to establish his position in your family pack. If you were able to set some rules in earlier stages of development, this won't be quite so difficult. However, if you cave in to that adorable puppy face, this could be a challenging time!

Discipline is necessary at any age, but will be especially important during 9 through 12 weeks of age. If you let your Bichon develop bad habits as a youngster, like digging in the garden, it will be harder to break him of these habits as he matures.

Photo by Isabelle Francais

Consistency in enforcing household rules is very important now, and everyone in the family or household should be enforcing the rules in the same way. Bichons are very perceptive, and if your puppy senses a weak link in the chain of command, he will take advantage of it. This doesn't mean he's a bad puppy, it simply means he's a smart puppy.

Puppies with dominant personalities may start mounting behavior on small children in the family or on the puppy's toys. Obviously, this is undesirable behavior and

Photo by Isabelle Francais

Let's play! Retrieving a favorite toy or chasing a ball is great exercise for a puppy and can teach him that he must play by your rules, which sets the stage for a solid working relationship with your pet.

RETRIEVING

Begin retrieving games at 9 to 12 weeks of age. Get your Bichon's attention with a toy he likes, and then toss it four to six feet away. When he grabs the toy, call him back to you in a happy tone of voice. Praise him enthusiastically when he brings it back to you. If he runs away and tries to get you to chase him, stand up and walk away, stopping the game completely. Let him learn now, while he's young, that he must play games by your rules. Chasing a ball or soft flying disc can be great exercise for the puppy and teaching him to play by your rules sets the stage for a sound working relationship later.

should be stopped immediately. Just don't let it happen!

Socialization to other people and friendly dogs, and exposure to new experiences should continue throughout this stage of development.

WEEKS SEVENTEEN THROUGH TWENTY SIX

Sometime between 17 and 26 weeks of age, most puppies go through another fear period, much like the one they went through at 8 weeks of age. Things the puppy had accepted as normal may suddenly become frightening. A friend's

Bichon walked into the backyard and began barking fearfully at a large potted plant that had been there in the same spot since before the puppy joined the family. The only difference was that the plant had begun to bloom, and all at once it was very scary!

Make sure you don't reinforce any of these fears. If you pet him or cuddle him and tell him softly, "It's okay, sweetie, don't be afraid," he will assume these are positive reinforcements for his fears. In other words, your puppy will think he was right to be afraid. Instead, walk up to whatever is scaring him, letting him see you touch it, as you tell him, "Look at this!" Use a happy, fun, playful tone of voice so that he can see the thing he is afraid of really isn't scary at all.

THE TEENAGE MONTHS

The teenage months in dogs are very much like the teenage years in human children. Human adolescents are feeling strong and striving to prove their ability to take care of themselves. They want to be independent, yet they still want the security of home. These two conflicting needs seem to drive some teens (and their parents) absolutely crazy.

Dogs can be very much the same way. Bichons in adolescence push the boundaries of their rules, trying to see if you really will enforce those rules. Most Bichon owners say their dogs in this stage of growing up act "too full of themselves!"

The teenage stage in Bichons usually hits at about 12 months of age, although it's not unusual to see it happen a month or two earlier. You'll know when it happens. One day you will ask your previously well-trained dog to do something he knows

A puppy should not be forced into a situation he finds frightening. Respect his feelings and allow him to acclimate by giving him time and reassurance.

Photo by Vince Serbin

Although your adolescent Bichon may try to assert his independence by breaking some rules, he must learn that you are the boss. Consistency in enforcing household rules is very important now.

very well, such as sit, and he'll look at you as if you're nuts. He's never heard that word before in his life, and even if he had, he still wouldn't do it.

Other common behaviors include a regression in social skills. Your previously well-socialized Bichon may start barking at other dogs or jumping on people. He may get rough with children or start chasing the cat.

During this stage of development, you must consistently enforce social and household rules. Hopefully you will have already started obedience training, because that control will help. If you haven't started obedience training, don't wait any longer.

Make sure, too, that your dog regards you as the leader. This is not the time to try to be best friends—that would cause a dominant personality to regard you as weak. Instead, act like the leader. Stand tall when you relate to your dog. Bend over him, not down to him, when you pet him. You should always go first through doorways or up the stairs—make him wait and follow you. You should always eat first before you feed him.

As the leader, you can give him permission to do things. For example, if he goes to pick up a toy for you to throw for him, give him permission to do it, "Good boy to bring me your toy!" If he lies down at your feet (by his own choice), tell him, "Good boy to lie down!" By giving him permission and praising him, you are putting yourself in control, even though he was already doing it of his own accord.

You need to understand that this rebellion is not aimed toward you, personally. Your Bichon is not doing this *to* you. Instead, it is a very natural part of growing up. Keep in mind that this, too, shall pass. Your Bichon will grow up, someday. Adolescence usually only lasts a few months (in dogs, anyway).

Growing Up

Bichons are not usually considered fully mature—mentally and physically—until they are two years old. And even then, some Bichons still act like puppies for even longer. Usually, the bitches (females) act mature a little earlier than the males.

After the teenage stage but before maturity, your Bichon may go through another fear period. This usually hits at about 14 months of age but may be later. Handle this one just like you did the others—don't reinforce your dog's fears. Happily, this is usually the last fear stage your dog will have.

There may be another period of challenging—seeing if you really are the boss—at about two years of age. Treat this as you did the teenage stage: Enforce the rules and praise what he does right.

When your Bichon reaches his third birthday, throw a party! He is usually considered grown up now. However, grown up to a Bichon doesn't mean life is serious—life for a Bichon is always fun!

Bichons are not usually considered fully mature—physically or mentally—until they are two years old.

Photo by Robert Smith

Early
PUPPY
Training

CRATE TRAINING

By about five weeks of age, most puppies are starting to toddle away from their mom and littermates to relieve themselves. You can use this instinct to keep the bed clean to your advantage, and with the help of a crate, you can housetrain your Bichon puppy. A crate is a plastic or wire travel cage that you will use as your Bichon's bed. For most Bichons, I advise using a solid-sided plastic crate (rather than the open-sided wire ones), because the solid sides give the puppy an illusion of more security.

Many new Bichon owners shudder at the thought of putting their puppy in a cage. "I could never do that!" they say, "It would be like putting my child

Teach your Bichon as a puppy what you want him to do as an adult. What he learns in his early months will have bearing on his behavior for the rest of his life.

Photo by Isabelle Francais

in jail!" A puppy is not a child, however, and he has different needs and instincts. Puppies like to curl up in small dark places. That's why they like to sleep under the coffee table or under a chair.

Because your Bichon puppy has an instinct to keep his bed clean, being confined in the crate will help him to develop more bowel and bladder control. When he is confined for gradually extended periods of time, he will hold his wastes to avoid soiling his bed. It is your responsibility to make sure he isn't left in the crate too long.

The crate will also be your Bichon puppy's place of refuge. If

Crate training is the easiest and fastest way to housetrain your Bichon puppy.

he's tired, hurt, or sick, allow him to go back to his crate to sleep or hide. If he's overstimulated or excited, put him back in his crate to calm down.

Because the crate physically confines the puppy, it can also prevent some unwanted behaviors such as destructive chewing or raiding the trash cans—behaviors that tempt many Bichons. When you cannot supervise the puppy or when you leave the house, put him in his crate and he won't be able to get into trouble.

Introducing the Crate

Introduce your puppy to the crate by propping open the door and tossing a treat inside. As you do this, tell your puppy, "Go to bed!" Let him go inside

Begin introducing your Bichon to his crate by offering him treats or several meals there. This will show him that it's a pretty neat place to go.

to get the treat. Let him investigate the crate and come and go as he wishes. When he's comfortable with that, offer him his next meal in the crate. Once he's in, close the door behind him. Let him out when he's through eating. Offer several meals in the same fashion to show your puppy that the crate is a pretty neat place.

After your Bichon is used to going in and out for treats and meals, start feeding him in the normal location again and go back to offering a treat for going into the crate. Tell him, "Sweetie, go to bed," and then give him his treat.

Don't let your puppy out of the crate for a temper tantrum. If he starts crying, screaming, throwing himself at the door, or scratching at the door, correct him verbally, "No, quiet!" or simply close the door to the room and walk away. If you let him out after a tantrum, you will simply teach him that temper tantrums work. Instead, let him out when you are ready to let him out and when he is quiet.

Crate Location
The ideal place for the crate is in your bedroom, within arm's reach of the bed. This will give your Bichon eight uninterrupted

The ideal place for a crate is in your bedroom—having you nearby during the night will give your Bichon puppy a feeling of security, whereas exiling him to another room will make him feel afraid and lonely.

Photo by Isabelle Francais

If you take your puppy to the same place to eliminate every time, he will know what's expected of him. Reinforce what he has learned by praising him when he relieves himself in the correct area.

hours with you while you do nothing but sleep. In these busy times, that is quality time.

Having you nearby will give your Bichon puppy a feeling of security, whereas exiling him to the laundry room or backyard will isolate him. He will be more apt to cry, whine, chew destructively, or get into other trouble because of loneliness and fear.

Having the crate close at night will save you some wear and tear, too. If he needs to go outside during the night (and he may need to for a few weeks), you will hear him whine, and you can let him out before he has an accident. If he's restless or bored, you can rap on the top of his crate and tell him to be quiet without getting out of bed.

HOUSETRAINING

One of the most common methods of housetraining a puppy is paper training. The puppy is taught to relieve himself on newspapers and then at some point is retrained to go outside. Paper training teaches the puppy to relieve himself in the house. Is that really what you want your Bichon to know? Teach your Bichon what you want him to know now *and* later as an adult.

Take him outside to the place where you want him to relieve himself and tell him, "Sweetie, go potty." (Use any word you'll be comfortable saying.) When he has done what he needs to do, praise him. Don't just open the door and send your puppy outside. How do you know that he has relieved himself? Go out with him so that you can teach him the command, praise him when he does it, and know that he is done and that it's safe to let him back inside.

If he doesn't relieve himself when you take him outside, just put him back in his crate for a little while and take him back outside later. Do *not* let him run around the house, even supervised, if he has not relieved himself outside.

Successful housetraining is based on setting your Bichon puppy up for success rather than

PUNISHMENT

Do not try to housetrain your puppy by correcting him for relieving himself in the house. If you scold him or rub his nose in his mess, you are not teaching him *where* he needs to relieve himself. Instead, you are teaching him that you think going potty is wrong. Since he *has* to go, he will then become sneaky about it, and you will find puddles and piles in strange places. Keep in mind that the act of relieving himself is very natural—he has to do it. So instead of concentrating on correction, emphasize praise for going in the right place.

failure. Keep accidents to a minimum, and praise him when he relieves himself in the appropriate location.

Bichons are creatures of habit and thrive on routine, so to make training easier, set a schedule for eating, elimination, playing, walking, and sleeping.

Photo by Robert Pearcy

b i c h o n   f r i s e

Photo by Isabelle Francais

Successful training relies not only on your ability to establish rules for your puppy, but also on setting him up for success rather than failure.

bichon frise

Establish a Routine

Bichons, like many other dogs, are creatures of habit and thrive on a routine. Housetraining is much easier if there is a set routine for eating, eliminating, playing, walking, training, and sleeping. A workable schedule might look like this:

• **6:00 am**—Dad wakes up and takes the puppy outside. After the puppy relieves himself, Dad praises him and brings him inside. Dad fixes the puppy's breakfast, offers him water, and then sends him out in the backyard while Dad goes to take his shower.

• **7:00 am**—Mom goes outside to play with the puppy for a few minutes before getting ready for work. Just before she leaves, she brings the puppy inside, puts him in his crate, and gives him a treat.

• **11:00 am**—A dog-loving neighbor who is retired comes over. He lets the puppy out of his crate and takes him outside. The neighbor is familiar with the puppy's training, so he praises the puppy when he relieves himself. He throws the ball for the puppy, pets him, and cuddles him. When the puppy is worn out, he puts him back in his crate and gives him a treat.

• **3:00 pm**—Daughter comes home from school and takes the puppy outside. She throws the ball for the puppy, cleans up the yard a little, and then takes the puppy for a walk. When they get back, she brings the puppy inside to her bedroom while she does her homework.

• **6:00 pm**—Mom takes the puppy outside to go potty,

It is important to give your puppy time to learn and time to grow up. If you stick to a schedule, your puppy will progress.

Photo by Isabelle Francais

THERE ARE NO ACCIDENTS

If the puppy relieves himself in the house it is not his fault, it's yours. It means the puppy was not supervised well enough or he wasn't taken outside in time. The act of relieving himself is very natural to the puppy, and the idea that there are certain areas where relieving himself is *not* acceptable is foreign to him. His instincts tell him to keep his bed clean, but that's all. You need to teach him where you want him to go and prevent him from going in other places. That requires your supervision.

praises him, and then feeds him dinner.

• **8:00 pm**—After Daughter plays with the puppy, she brushes him and takes him outside to go potty.

• **11:00 pm**—Dad takes the puppy outside for one last trip before bed.

The schedule you set up will have to work with your normal routine and lifestyle. Just keep in mind that your Bichon puppy should not remain in the crate for longer than three to four hours at a time, except during the night. In addition, the puppy will need to relieve himself after waking up, eating, playtime, and every three to four hours in between.

Limit the Puppy's Freedom

Many puppies do not want to take the time to go outside to relieve themselves because everything exciting happens in the house. After all, that's where all the family members are. If your Bichon puppy is like this, you will find him sneaking off somewhere—behind the sofa or to another room—to relieve himself. By limiting the puppy's freedom, you can prevent some of these mistakes. Close bedroom doors and use baby gates across hallways to keep him close. If you can't keep an eye on him, put him in his crate or outside.

By limiting your puppy's freedom, you can prevent accidents from occurring. If you can't supervise your Bichon, put him in his crate or outside in a fenced area.

Photo by Isabelle Francais

PATIENCE, PATIENCE, AND MORE PATIENCE

Bichon puppies need time to develop bowel and bladder control. Establish a routine that seems to work well for you and your puppy, and then stick to it. Give your puppy time to learn what you want and time to grow up. If you stick to the schedule, your puppy will progress. However, don't let success go to your head. A few weeks without a mistake doesn't mean your Bichon puppy is housetrained; it means your routine is working! Too much freedom too soon will result in problems.

HOUSEHOLD RULES

It's important to start teaching your Bichon puppy the household rules that you wish him to observe as soon as possible. Your eight- to ten-week-old puppy is not too young to learn, and by starting early, you can prevent him from learning bad habits.

Some rules you may want to institute could include teaching your Bichon that jumping on people is not allowed, that he must behave when guests come to the house, that he should stay out of the kitchen, that he should leave the trash cans alone, and that he should chew only on his toys.

Teaching your Bichon puppy these rules is not difficult. Be very clear with your corrections. When he does something wrong, correct him with a deep, firm tone of voice, "No jump!" When he does

You can keep your Bichon from learning bad habits by beginning obedience training early—your eight-to-ten-week old puppy is not too young to learn.

Photo by Isabelle Francais

KEEP WALKING

Do you walk your dog when he has to go potty? Many dog owners live in condos and apartments, and the dog must go for a walk to relieve himself. These dogs often learn that the walk is over once they go potty, and they hold it as long as possible so that the walk continues. To avoid this trap, encourage your puppy to relieve himself right away, praise him, and then continue the walk or outing for a little while afterward.

something right, use a high-pitched tone of voice, "Good boy to chew on your toy!" You must be very clear—either something is right or it is wrong, there are no shades of gray in between.

ACCEPTING THE LEASH

Learning to accept the leash can be difficult for some puppies. If your Bichon puppy learns to dislike the leash as a young puppy, he may continue to resent it for many years. However, if he learns the leash is a key to more exciting things, he will welcome the leash.

Soon after you bring your puppy home, put a soft, buckle collar on his neck. Make sure it's loose enough to come over his head if he gets tangled up in something. Give him a day or two to get used to the collar. Then, when you are going to be close by and can supervise him, snap the leash onto the collar and let him drag it behind him.

Your Bichon must learn to accept a collar and leash for his safety as well as the safety of others.

bichon frise

As he walks around, he will step on the leash, feel it tug on his neck, and get used to the feel of it.

After two or three short sessions like this, you can teach your puppy to follow you on the leash. Have a few pieces of a soft, easily chewed treat your puppy enjoys. Hold the leash in one hand and the treats in another. Show him the treat and back away a few steps as

If your Bichon likes to pull you along when he's on leash, try a no-pull training halter, guaranteed by the manufacturer to stop any dog, any size, any weight from pulling. Photo courtesy of Four Paws.

Four Paws®
NO-PULL
TRAINER
see back panel for size chart.
Large
FOR MAXIMUM CONTROL
WITHOUT CHOKING YOUR DOG

STOPS ANY DOG
FROM PULLING

The No-Pull Trainer is guaranteed to stop any dog, any size from pulling or your money back from manufacturer

Item #59225

you tell your puppy, "Let's go! Good boy!" When he follows you a few steps, praise him and give him the treat. Bichon puppies are usually very food-motivated, and when he learns a treat is being offered, he should follow you with no problem. Repeat two or three times and then stop the training session. Reward your puppy by giving him a tummy rub or by throwing the ball a few times.

After two or three training session like this, make it more challenging by backing up slowly, quickly, or by making turns. If he gets confused or balks, make it simple again until he's willingly following you.

INTRODUCING THE CAR

Many puppies are afraid of the car because a ride in the car was the first strange thing to happen to them when they were taken from their mother and littermates. The car also takes them to the veterinarian's office, another strange place where someone in a white coat pokes them, prods them, and gives them shots. You don't want this fear of the car to grab hold, though. Your puppy should understand that riding in the car is something fun to do.

Photo by Isabelle Francais

Patience, praise, and affection are the best motivators for your Bichon.

Start by lifting your puppy into the car and handing him a treat. As soon as he finishes the treat, lift him down and walk away. Repeat this simple exercise several times a day for a few days. Then lift him into the car, give him a treat, let him eat it, and then let him explore the car for a few minutes. After he has sniffed for a while, give him another treat, let him eat it, then lift him down and walk away. Continue this training for a week or two, depending on how nervous your puppy is in the car.

When your puppy is expecting a treat in the car, put his crate in the car and strap it down securely. Put your puppy in his crate, give him a treat and

---

IF YOUR PUPPY BALKS

If your puppy balks, do not use the leash to drag him to you. This will cause him to dig his feet in and apply the brakes. Instead, kneel down, open your arms wide, and encourage him to come to you by saying, "Hey, Sweetie, here! Good boy!" When he dashes to your lap, praise him and tell him what a wonderful puppy he is. Then try the exercise again.

Photo by Vince Serbin

Once your Bichon is used to being handled, it will be easier to attend to his grooming needs and to keep on top of his physical condition.

then start the car's engine. Back down the driveway and then back up to the house. Stop the engine, give your puppy a treat, and let him out of his crate and the car.

The next time, drive down the street and back. Then go around the block. Increase the distances and times of the drives very gradually. Keep in mind, you want your puppy to expect good things in the car, not scary things. Your Bichon puppy will have a lifetime of car rides ahead of him, and life will be much nicer if he enjoys the rides.

SOCIAL HANDLING

Your Bichon puppy cannot care for himself. You must be able to brush and comb him, bathe him, check his feet for cuts and scrapes, and clean his

END ON A HIGH NOTE

Always end these (and all) training sessions on a high note. If your Bichon puppy is worried, scared, and confused, help him do something right and then end the training session with that praise. Never end the training session at a negative point in the training, or it will affect his outlook toward training later.

ears. Your Bichon puppy doesn't understand why you need to do these annoying things to him, and he may struggle when you try to care for him. This social handling exercise will help teach your puppy to accept your care.

Sit down on the floor with your puppy and have him lie down between your legs. He can lie on his back or on his side—let him get comfortable. Start by giving him a slow, easy tummy rub. The idea here is to relax him. If your movements are fast and vigorous, you'll make him want to play. Keep it slow and gentle. If he starts to struggle, tell him calmly, "Easy.

Photo by Isabelle Francais

Learning good manners and obedience skills can help ensure that your Bichon will become a treasured member of the family for years to come.

Be still." Restrain him gently if you need to do so.

When your puppy is relaxed, start giving him a massage. Start at his neck and ears, gently rubbing all around the base of each ear and working down the neck to the shoulders. Continue over his body, gently massaging it, while at the same time you check his body for tangles in his coat, mats, cuts, scratches, lumps, bumps, bruises, fleas, ticks, or any other problems that need to be taken care of.

Once your puppy has learned to enjoy this handling, you can clean his ears, wash out his eyes, trim his toenails, or do anything else that needs to be done during the massage.

RELAX!

You can also use the social handling exercise to relax your puppy when he's overstimulated. If you let him in from the backyard and he's full of Bichon energy, don't chase him down or try to correct him. Instead, sit down on the floor and invite him to join you. (Use a treat to get him to come to you if you need some extra incentive.) Once he's come to you, lay him down and begin the massage. He will relax and calm down, and in the process, you are also giving him the attention he needs from you.

The Basic
OBEDIENCE
Commands

WHY IS TRAINING IMPORTANT?

When you decided to add a Bichon to your family, you probably did so because you wanted a companion, a friend, and a confidant. You may have wanted a dog to go for walks, run along the beach, catch tennis balls, and hike in the mountains with you. You may have wanted your children to have the same relationship with a dog that you remember from your childhood. To do any of these things, your Bichon will need training.

Many dog owners, especially the owners of small dogs, won't admit their dog needs training. "He does everything I ask," they say. Yet when asked specific questions about behavior, the answer changes. A trained Bichon won't jump up on people, dash out the open door, or raid the trash can.

Dog owners benefit from training, too. During training, you learn how to teach your Bichon and how to motivate him to be good so that you can

Dog owners benefit from training, too. During obedience training, you learn how to teach your Bichon so that you can encourage good behavior and prevent problems.

Photo by Isabelle Francais

Use only as much correction as is needed to get your puppy's attention and remember to correct only when he makes a mistake, not after.

encourage good behavior. You also learn how to prevent problem behavior from happening and how to correct the inevitable mistakes.

THE TEACHING PROCESS

Bichon Frises are a very intelligent breed. However, they are known for having a mind of their own and just a little bit of a stubborn streak! Training a Bichon requires you to keep the training upbeat, as positive as possible, and just firm enough to let the dog know that you require him to behave himself.

Show Your Dog

First of all, you want to show your dog what it is you want him to do and that there is a word—a human spoken sound—associated with that action or position. For example, when teaching him to sit, you can help him into position as you tell him, "Sweetie, sit." Follow that with praise—"Good boy to sit!"—even if you helped him into position. You will follow the same pattern when teaching your dog most new things. If you want him off the sofa, you can tell him, "Sweetie, off the furniture," as you take him by the collar and pull him off. When he's off the furniture, tell him, "Good boy to get off the furniture."

Praise

Praise him every time he does something right, even if

you help him do it. Your Bichon will pay more attention and try harder if he is praised for his efforts. However, don't praise him when it's undeserved. Bichons are very intelligent dogs and will quickly figure this out. Instead, give enthusiastic praise when he makes an effort and does something right for you. If your dog gets too excited by enthusiastic praise (as some Bichons do), tone it down just a little.

Correct

Do not correct your dog until he understands what you want him to do. After he understands and is willing to obey the command, then chooses *not* to do it, you can correct him verbally, "Sweetie, no!" or give him a quick snap and release of the collar. Use *only* as much correction as is needed to get his attention. With corrections, less is usually better as long as your dog is responding.

Your Timing

The timing of your praise, corrections, and interruptions is very important. Praise him *as* he is doing something right. Correct him *when* he makes

The basic obedience commands can be used to stop undesirable behavior—like jumping up on furniture or chewing on your favorite book!

the mistake. Interrupt him *as* he starts to stick his nose into the trash can. If your timing is slow, he may not understand what you are trying to teach him.

Be Fair

Bichons resent corrections that are too harsh or unfair. They will show this resentment by refusing to work, by planting themselves and refusing to move, or by fighting back. Some Bichons will even show signs of depression if a harsh training method continues.

Interruptions and corrections alone will not teach your Bichon. They are used to stop undesirable behavior or actions at the precise moment they occur. When you reward good behavior, your Bichon learns what you want him to do. Stop the behavior you don't want, but lavishly praise the actions you want to continue.

The sit is the foundation command for everything else your dog will learn. This obedient Bichon demonstrates a perfect sit.

THE BASIC COMMANDS

Sit and Release

The sit is the foundation command for everything else your Bichon will learn. When your Bichon learns to sit still, he learns to control himself and that there are consequences to his actions. This is a very big lesson.

Sitting is also a good alternative action for problem behavior. Your Bichon cannot both sit still and jump on you. He can only do one or the other, so learning to sit still for

---

USE INTERRUPTIONS

Interrupt incorrect behavior as you see it happen. If your dog is walking by the kitchen trash can and turns to sniff it, interrupt him, "Leave it alone!" If you tell him to sit and he does sit, but then starts to get up, interrupt him, "No! Sit." By interrupting him, you can stop incorrect behavior before or as it happens.

---

praise can replace jumping up on people for attention. He can't knock his food bowl out of your hand if he's sitting still, waiting patiently for his dinner. You can fasten his leash to his collar more easily if he's sitting still. This is a practical, useful command.

There are two basic methods of teaching your Bichon to sit. Some dogs do better with one technique than the other, so try both and see which is better for your Bichon.

Hold your Bichon's leash in your left hand and have some treats in your right hand. Tell your Bichon, "Sweetie, sit!" as you move your right hand (with the treats) from his nose over his head toward his tail. He will lift his head to watch your hand. As his head goes up and back, his hips will go down. As he sits, praise him, "Good boy to sit!" and give him a treat. Pet him in the sitting position.

When you are ready for him to get up, tap him on the shoulder as you tell him, "Release!" Each exercise needs a beginning and an end. The sit command is the beginning, and the release command tells him

---

SIT, PLEASE!

Once your Bichon understand the sit command and is responding well, start having him sit for things that he wants. Have him sit before you hook his leash to his collar for a walk, give him a treat, give him his meals, or throw his ball.

Teach your Bichon to sit by holding a treat in your hand and moving it from his head toward his tail. As his head goes up to follow your hand, his hips will go down into a sit.

Photo by Isabelle Francais

bichon frise

When teaching the down exercise, start with your Bichon in the sit/stay position, then have him follow a treat to the ground as you give the command. Let him have the treat when he reaches the down position.

he is done and can move now. If he doesn't get up on his own, use your hands on his collar to walk him forward.

If your Bichon is too excited by the treats to think (and some Bichons are like that, especially in the early stages of training), put the treats away. Tell your Bichon to sit as you place one hand under his chin on the front

of the neck and slide the other hand down his hips to tuck his back legs under. Gently shape him into a sit as you give him the command, "Sweetie, sit." Praise and release him.

If your dog is wiggly as you try to teach this exercise, keep your hands on him. If he pops up, interrupt that action with a deep, firm tone of voice, "Be still!" When he responds and stops wiggling, praise him quietly and gently.

ONE COMMAND

Don't keep repeating any command. The command is not, "Sit! Sit, sit, *sit,* please sit. SIT!!" If you give repeated commands to sit, your Bichon will assume that this carries over to everything else. Tell him one time to sit and then help him do it.

Down

The down exercise continues one of the lessons the sit command started, that of self-control. It is hard for many energetic, bouncy young

> **BE CLEAR**
>
> Be sure you make it very clear to your dog what you want him to do. Remember, something is either right or wrong to your dog—it's not partly right or partly wrong. Be fair with your commands, your praise, and your corrections.

Bichons to control their own actions, but it is a lesson all must learn. Practicing the down exercise teaches your Bichon to lie down and be still.

Start with your Bichon in a sit. Rest one hand gently on his shoulder and have a treat in the other hand. Let him smell the treat and then tell him, "Sweetie, down," taking the treat straight down to the ground in front of his front paws. As he follows the treat down, use your hand on his shoulders to encourage him to lie down. Praise him, give him the treat, and then have him hold the position for a moment. Then release him in the same way you did from the sit: Pat him on the shoulder, tell him "Release!" and let him get up.

If your dog looks at the treat as you make the signal but doesn't follow the treat to the ground, simply scoop

his front legs up and forward as you lay him down. The rest of the exercise is the same.

As your Bichon learns what the down command means, you can have him hold it for a few minutes longer before you release him, but do not step away from him yet. Stay next to him, and if he's wiggly, keep a hand on his shoulder to help him stay in position.

Once each day, have your Bichon lie down and then, before you release him, roll him over for a tummy rub. He will enjoy the tummy rub, relax a little, and will learn to enjoy the down position. This is especially important for young Bichons that want to do anything *but* lie down and hold still.

Stay

When your Bichon understands both the sit and down commands, you can introduce him to the stay exercise. You want to convey to your Bichon that the word "stay" means "hold still." When your dog is sitting and you tell him to stay, you want him to remain in the sitting position until you go back to him and release him. When you tell him to stay while he's lying down, you want him to

Aside from having very practical uses, the stay command teaches your dog self-control—so you can have your Bichon accompany you wherever you go.

same time, release the pressure on the leash.

If your dog moves or gets up, tell him "No!" so that he knows he made a mistake and put him back into position. Repeat the exercise. After a few seconds, go back to him and praise him. Don't let him move from position until you release him. Use the same process to teach the stay in the down position.

With the stay commands, you always want to go back to your Bichon to release him. Don't release him from a distance or call him to come from the stay. If

remain lying down until you go back to him to release him from that position. Eventually, he will be able to hold the sit position for several minutes and the down for even longer.

Start by having your Bichon sit. With the leash in your left hand, use the leash to put a slight bit of pressure backward (toward his tail) as you tell him, "Sweetie, stay." At the same time, use your right hand to give your dog a hand signal that will mean stay— an open-handed gesture with the palm toward your dog's face. Take one step away, and at the

Hand signals used in conjunction with verbal commands can be very effective when teaching your Bichon basic obedience. This open-handed gesture with the palm toward your dog's face means stay.

you do either of these, your dog will be much less reliable on the stay. He will continue to get up from the stay because you will have taught him to do exactly that. When teaching the stay, you want your Bichon to learn that stay means "Hold this position until I come back to you to release you."

As your Bichon learns the stay command, you can *gradually* increase the time you ask him to hold it. However, if your dog is making a lot of mistakes and moving often, you are either asking your dog to hold it too long or your dog doesn't understand the command yet. In either case, go back and reteach the exercise from the beginning.

Increase the distance from your dog very gradually, too. Again, if your dog is making a lot of mistakes, you're moving away too quickly. Teach everything very gradually.

When your Bichon understands the stay command but chooses not to do it, you need to let him know the command is not optional. Many young, wiggly Bichons want to do anything except hold still, but holding still is very important to Bichon owners! Correct excess movement first with your voice: "No! Be still! Stay!" and if that doesn't

> **USING THE STAY COMMAND**
> You can use the stay command around the house. For example, in the evening while you're watching a favorite television show, have your Bichon lie down at your feet while you sit on the sofa. Give him a toy to chew on and tell him, "Sweetie, stay." Have him do a down/stay when your guests visit so he isn't jumping all over them. Have him lie down and stay while the family is eating so he isn't begging under the table. There are a lot of practical uses for the stay— just look at your normal routine and see where this command can work for you.

stop the excess movement, use a verbal correction and a snap and release of the leash. When he does control himself, praise him enthusiastically.

Watch Me

The "watch me" exercise teaches your Bichon to ignore distractions and pay attention to you. This is particularly useful when you're out in public and your dog is distracted by children playing or dogs barking behind a fence. Start by having your Bichon sit in front of you. Have a treat in your right hand. Let him sniff the treat and then tell him, "Sweetie, watch me!"

as you take the treat from his nose up to your chin. When his eyes follow the treat in your hand and he looks at your face, praise him, "Good boy to watch me!" and give him the treat. Then release him from the sit. Repeat it again exactly the same way two or three times and then end the training session.

Because this is hard for young, bouncing Bichons, practice it first at home when there are few distractions. However, once he knows it well inside, you then need to try it with distractions. Take him out in the front yard (on his leash, of course), and tell him to watch you. If he ignores you, take his chin in your left hand (the treat is in the right hand) and hold his chin so that he has to look at your face. Praise him even though you are helping him do it.

When he will watch you out front with some distractions, move on to the next step. Have him sit in front of you and tell him to watch you. As he watches you, take a few steps backward and ask him to follow you and watch you at the same time. Praise him when he does. Try it again. When he can follow you six or seven steps and watch you at the same time, make it more challenging—back up and turn to the left or right or back up more

quickly. Praise him when he continues to watch you.

Heel

You want your Bichon to learn that heel means, "walk by my left side, with your neck and shoulders by my left leg, and maintain that position." Ideally, your Bichon should maintain that position as you walk slowly, quickly, turn corners, or weave in and out through a crowd.

To start, practice a "watch me" exercise to get your dog's attention on you. Back away from him and encourage him to watch you. When he does, simply

Eye contact is an essential element in training. The "watch me" exercise teaches your Bichon to ignore distractions and focus on you.

Photo by Isabelle Francais

The heel exercise teaches your dog to walk beside you without pulling, which will make your daily outings together more enjoyable.

turn your body as you are backing up so that your dog ends up on your left side, and continue walking. If you have done it correctly, it is one smooth movement so you and your dog end up walking forward together with your dog on your left side.

Let's repeat it in slow motion. Sit your dog in front of you and do a "watch me." Back away from your dog and encourage him to follow you. When he's watching you, back up toward your left, and as you are backing up, continue turning in that direction so you and your dog end up walking forward together. Your dog should end up on your left side and you should end up on your dog's right side.

If your dog starts to pull forward, simply back away from him and encourage him to follow you. If you need to do so, use the leash with a snap-and-release motion to make the dog follow you. Praise him when he does. Don't hesitate to go back and forth, walking forward and then backing away, if you need to do so. In fact, sometimes this can be the best exercise you can do to get your dog's attention on you.

When your dog is walking nicely with you and paying attention to you, then you can start eliminating the backing away. Start the heel with your Bichon sitting by your left side. Tell him, "Sweetie, watch me! Heel." Start walking. When he's walking nicely with you, praise him. However, if he gets distracted or starts to pull, simply back away from him again.

Come

The come command is one of the most important commands your Bichon needs to learn. Not only is the come command important around the house in your daily routine, but it could also be a lifesaver someday, especially if he should decide to dash toward the street when a car is coming. Because the come command is so important, you will use two different techniques to teach your dog to come to you when you call him.

Come with a Treat

The first technique will use a sound stimulus and a treat to teach your Bichon to come when you call him. Take a small plastic container (such as a margarine tub), and put a handful of dry dog food in it. Put the lid on and shake it. It should make a nice rattling sound.

Have the shaker in one hand and some good dog treats in the other. Shake the container, and as your Bichon looks at it and you, ask him, "Sweetie, cookie?" Use whatever word he already knows for treat. When you say

USING A SOUND STIMULUS

Do you remember those silent dog whistles that used to be advertised in comic books? There was nothing magical about those whistles except that they were so high-pitched, dogs could hear them but people couldn't. The container we're using for teaching the come command works on the same principle that the silent dog whistle used—it's a sound stimulus you can use to get the dog's attention so that you can teach him. By teaching him to pay attention to the sound of the shaker, and by teaching him that the sound of the shaker means he's going to get a treat, we can make coming when called that much more exciting. Your dog will be more likely to come to you, especially when there are distractions, if he's excited about it.

The come command is one of the most important commands your Bichon needs to learn; it could also be a lifesaver someday.

Photo by Robert Pearcy

bichon frise

However, you are teaching him that the sound of the shaker now equals the word "come" and he still gets the treat. Practice this several times a day for several days.

When your Bichon is happy to hear the shaker and is drooling to get a treat, start calling him across the room. Shake the container as you say, "Sweetie, come!" When he dashes to you, continue to give him a treat as you praise him, "Good boy to come!" Practice this up and

In the early stages of training, treats are a great way to motivate your Bichon to learn. Once he knows the basic commands, you can wean him from the treats.

"cookie," pop a treat in his mouth. Do it again. Shake, shake, say, "Sweetie, cookie?" and pop a treat in his mouth.

The sound of the container, your verbal question, and the treat are all becoming associated in his mind. He is learning that the sound of the container equals the treat, an important lesson! Do this several times a day for several days.

Then, with him sitting in front of you, replace the word "cookie" with the word "come." Shake the container, say, "Sweetie, come!" and pop a treat in his mouth. You are rewarding him even though he didn't actually come to you—he was still sitting in front of you.

Photo by Isabelle Francais

down the hallway, inside and outside, and across the backyard. Make it fun, keeping up with the treats and the verbal praise.

Come With a Long Line

The second method you'll use to teach your dog to come uses a long leash or a length of clothesline rope. Although Bichons are small dogs, they are very fast, so use a line at least 20 to 30 feet in length. Fasten the line to your Bichon's collar and then let him go play. When he is distracted by something, call him with "Sweetie, come!" If he responds and comes right away, praise him.

If he doesn't respond right away, do *not* call him again. Pick up the line, back away from him, and use the line to make

> **DON'T USE THE COME COMMAND TO PUNISH**
> Never call your dog to come and then punish him for something he did earlier. Not only is the late punishment ineffective (it always is), but that unfair punishment will teach your dog to avoid you when you call him. Always keep the come command positive.

him come to you. Do not give him a verbal correction at this time, because he may associate the verbal correction with coming to you. Instead, simply make him come to you even if you have to drag him in with the line.

Let him go again, and repeat the entire exercise. Make sure you always praise him when he does decide to come to you. If

Reinforce training commands whenever you can. For example, have your Bichon perform a sit/stay while you're chatting with a neighbor and her pets.

Photo by Isabelle Francais

Never allow your Bichon off-leash freedom until he reliably and consistently obeys your commands.

he is really distracted, use the shaker and treats along with the long line, especially in the early stages of the training. You can always wean him from the treats later—right now the goal is to make the come command work.

Don't allow your Bichon to have freedom off the leash until he is grown up enough to handle the responsibility and is very well trained. Many dog owners let their dog off leash much too soon and the dogs learn bad habits their owners wish they hadn't learned. Each time you allow your dog to ignore you or run away from you, it reinforces the fact that he can. Instead, let him run around and play while

dragging the long line. That way, you can always regain control when you need it.

USE IT OR LOSE IT!

The best way to make training work for you and your Bichon is to use it. Training is not just for training sessions; instead, training is for your daily life. Incorporate it into your daily routine. Have your Bichon sit before you feed him. Have him lie down and stay while you eat. Have him sit and stay at the gate while you take the trash cans out. Have him do a down/stay when guests come over. Use these commands as part of your life. They will work much better that way.

When teaching the come command, you can use a long line or retractable leash. It will provide the dog with freedom, while allowing the owner complete control. Leashes are available in a wide variety of lengths for all breeds of dog. Photo courtesy of Flexi-USA, Inc.

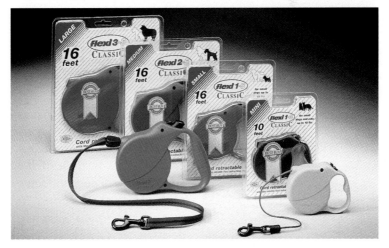

All About
FORMAL
Training

Formal dog training is much more than the traditional sit, down, stay, and come commands. Dog training means teaching your Bichon that he's living in your house, not his. It means you can set some rules and expect him to follow them. It will not turn your Bichon into a robot—instead, it will teach your Bichon to look at you in a new light. Training will cause you to look at him differently,

When looking for a training class, talk to instructors about their training methods and experience. Also, ask other pet owners for recommendations.

too. Training is not something you do *to* your Bichon, it's something you do together.

TRAINING METHODS

If you were to talk to 100 dog trainers (someone who trains dogs) or dog obedience instructors (someone who teaches the dog owner how to teach his dog) and ask them how they train, you would get 100 different answers. Any trainer or instructor who has been in the business for any period of time is going to work out a method or technique that works best for her. Each method will be based on the trainer's personality, teaching techniques, experience, and philosophy regarding dogs and dog training. Any method may work wonderfully for one trainer but fail terribly for another.

Because there are so many different techniques, styles, and methods, choosing a particular instructor may be difficult. It is important to understand some of the different methods so that you can make a reasonable decision.

Some Bichons would rather play than follow your rules—training can teach your dog to become a well-behaved companion that is a joy to spend time with.

Photo by Isabelle Francais

Compulsive Training

Compulsive training is a method of training that forces the dog to behave. This is usually a correction-based training style and sometimes uses forceful corrections. This training is usually used with law enforcement and military dogs and can be quite effective with hard-driving, strong-willed dogs. Many pet dog owners do not like this style of training, feeling it is too rough. It *is* too rough for most Bichons.

Inducive Training

This training is exactly the opposite of compulsive training. Instead of being forced to do something, the dog is induced or motivated toward proper behavior. Depending on the instructor, there are few or no corrections used. This training works very well for most puppies, softer dogs, and sometimes for owners who dislike corrections of any kind.

Unfortunately, this is not the right technique for all Bichons. Many Bichons will take advantage of the lack of corrections or discipline. Some very intelligent, very dominant-personality dogs (including some Bichons) look at the lack of discipline as weakness (on your part) and will then set their own rules which, unfortunately, may not be the rules you wish them to abide by. Also, because of their fun, happy-go-lucky personalities, without discipline or corrections, some Bichons would rather play than follow your rules.

Somewhere in the Middle

The majority of trainers and instructors use a training method that is somewhere in between these techniques. An inducive method is used when possible, while corrections are used when needed. Obviously, the range can be vast, with some trainers leaning toward more corrections and others using as few as possible.

GROUP CLASSES OR PRIVATE LESSONS?

There are benefits and drawbacks to both group classes and private lessons. In group classes, the dog must learn to behave around other distractions, specifically the other dogs and people in the class. Because the world is made up of lots of things capable of distracting your Bichon, this can work very well. A group class can also function as group therapy for dog owners. The owners can share triumphs and mishaps and can encourage and support one another. Many friendships have begun in group training classes.

The drawback to group classes is that for some dogs, the distractions of a group class are too much. Some dogs simply cannot concentrate at all, especially in the beginning

A group training class is a great way to learn basic obedience and a perfect place for your Bichon to improve his social skills.

Photo by Isabelle Francais.

Before you choose a training program, it is important to decide what you want to accomplish and to set goals for your Bichon.

of training. For these dogs, a few private lessons may help enough so that the dog can join a group class later. Dogs with severe behavior problems, especially aggression, should bypass group classes for obvious reasons.

Private lessons—one-on-one training with the owner, dog, and instructor—are also good for people with a very busy schedule who may otherwise not be able to do any training at all.

GOALS FOR YOUR BICHON

What do you want training to accomplish? Do you want your Bichon to be calm and well behaved around family members? Do you want him to behave himself out in public? Would you like to participate in dog activities and sports? There are an unlimited number of things you can do with your Bichon. It's up to you to decide what you would like to do. Then you can find a training program to help you achieve those goals. As you start training, talk to your trainer about them so she can guide you in the right direction.

Puppy Class

Puppy or kindergarten classes are for puppies older

than 10 weeks of age but not older than 16 weeks. These classes are usually half obedience training and half socialization, because for puppies, both of these subjects are very important. The puppy's owner also learns how to prevent problem behaviors from occurring and how to establish household rules.

Basic Obedience Class

This class is for puppies that have graduated from a puppy class, for puppies older than four months of age that haven't attended a puppy class, or for adult dogs. In this class, the dogs and their owners work on basic obedience commands

First-time dog owners should consider signing up for puppy classes. An experienced trainer can teach you how to prevent problem behaviors from occurring and how to establish household rules.

such as sit, down, stay, come, and heel. Most instructors also spend time discussing problem prevention and problem solving, especially the common problems like jumping on people, barking, digging, and chewing.

Dog Sports Training

Some instructors offer training for one or more of the various dog activities or sports. There are classes to prepare you for competition in obedience trials, conformation dog shows, flyball, or agility. Other trainers may offer training for noncompetitive activities such as therapy dog work.

Advanced Training

Advanced training classes vary depending on the instructor. Some offer classes to teach you to control your dog off leash, some emphasize dog sports, and others may simply continue basic training skills. Ask the instructor what she offers.

FINDING AN INSTRUCTOR OR TRAINER

When trying to find an instructor or trainer, word-of-mouth referrals are probably

Once your Bichon masters basic obedience, he can go on to compete in more advanced activities, like obedience trials or agility.

the best place to start. Although anyone can place an advertisement in the newspaper or yellow pages, the ad itself is no guarantee of quality or expertise. However, happy customers will demonstrate their experience with well-behaved dogs and will be glad to tell you where they received instruction.

Have you admired a neighbor's well-behaved dog? Ask where they went for training. Call your veterinarian, local pet store, or groomer, and ask who they recommend. Make notes about each referral. What did people like about this trainer? What did they dislike?

Once you have a list of referrals, call each instructor and ask a few questions: How long has she been teaching classes? You will want someone with experience, of course, so that she can handle the various situations that may arise. However, experience is not the only qualification. Some people that have been training for years are still teaching exactly the same way they did many years ago and have never learned anything new.

Ask the instructor about Bichons. What does she think of the breed? Ideally, she should be knowledgeable about the breed, what makes them tick,

Both you and your Bichon should feel comfortable with the instructor and his training methods.

and how to train them. If she doesn't like the breed, go elsewhere.

Ask the instructor to explain her training methods. Does this sound like something you would be comfortable with? Ask if there are alternative methods used. Not every dog will respond the same way, and every instructor should have a backup plan.

Does the instructor belong to any professional organizations? The National Association of Dog Obedience Instructors (NADOI) and the Association of Pet Dog Trainers (APDT) are two of the more prominent groups. Both of these organizations publish regular newsletters to share information, techniques, new developments, and more. Instructors belonging to organizations such as these are more likely to be up-to-date on training techniques, styles, and so forth, as well as information about specific dog breeds.

Make sure, too, that the instructor will be able to help you achieve your goals. For example, if you want to compete in obedience trials, the instructor should have experience in that field and knowledge of the rules and regulations of the competition.

After talking to several trainers or instructors, ask one if you can watch a training session or class. If she says no, then cross her off your list. There should be no reason why you cannot attend one class to see if you will be comfortable with this instructor and her style of teaching. As you watch the class, see how she handles students' dogs. Would you let her handle your dog? How does she relate to the students? Are they relaxed? Do they look like they're having a good time? Are they paying attention to her?

After talking to the instructor or trainer and after watching a class, you should be able to make a decision as to what class you want to attend. If you're still undecided, call the instructor back and ask a few more questions. After all, you are hiring her to provide a service, and you must be comfortable with your decision.

BUILDING A RELATIONSHIP

Training helps build a relationship between you and your dog. This relationship is built on mutual trust, affection, and respect. Training can help your dog become your best friend—a well-behaved companion that is a joy to spend time with and that won't send your blood pressure sky-high!

Advanced
TRAINING
and Dog Sports

If you enjoy training your Bichon, you never really have to stop. There is always something else you can do. I have owned a variety of breeds, large and small, and all of my dogs have learned and participated in a variety of different dog activities and sports. We do these things because I enjoy the training process, the companionship of my dogs as we both learn, and the fun we have together.

All of my dogs have been therapy dogs, a very worthwhile and rewarding activity. All of my dogs have learned to catch a Frisbee™. The bigger dogs even went on to compete in Frisbee™ competitions. My smaller dogs couldn't catch the regular sized Frisbee™, so we used the miniature four-inch flying discs. Agility trials are fun, and so is flyball. Carting or wagon-pulling can be useful as well as fun. There are tiny wagons made for small dogs, so even a Bichon can learn to pull a wagon. There are so many activities to try!

Bichons are athletic and highly trainable little dogs that thrive on physical activity. Participating in dog sports or competition is something you can enjoy together.

Photo by Isabelle Francais

bichon frise

Before beginning advanced training, your Bichon must be proficient in the basic commands. If he is having trouble, go back, review, and practice them. This Bichon demonstrates a perfect down/stay.

However, before you begin any of these exercises or activities, make sure your Bichon is proficient in all of the basic commands. If he's having trouble with some of the basic commands, go back and review and practice them.

HAND SIGNALS

When you start teaching hand signals, use a treat in your hand to get your Bichon's attention. Use the verbal command he already knows to help him understand what you are trying to tell him. As he begins to respond well, decrease the verbal command to a whisper and emphasize the hand signal.

The difficult part of teaching hand signals is that in the beginning, your dog may not understand that these movements of your hand and arm have any significance. After all, people "talk" with their hands all the time—hands are always moving and waving. Dogs learn early to ignore hand and arm movements. Therefore, to make hand signals work, your Bichon needs to watch you. A good treat in the hand making the movement can help.

Down

When you taught your Bichon to lie down by taking the treat from his nose to the ground in front of his front paws, you were teaching him a hand signal. Granted, he was watching the treat in your hand, but he was also getting used to seeing your hand move. Therefore, switching him over from a verbal command to a hand-signal-only command should be easy.

Have your dog sit in front of you. Verbally tell him, "Down" as you give him the hand signal for down with a treat in your hand, just as you did when you were originally teaching it. When he lies down, praise him and then release him. Practice this a few times.

Now, give him the signal to go down with a treat in your hand, but do not give a verbal command. If he lies down, praise him, give him the treat, and release him. If he does not go down, give the leash a slight snap and release down toward the ground—not hard, but just enough to let him know, "Hey! Pay attention!" When he goes down, praise and release him.

When he responds to the signal with no verbal command reliably, make it more challenging. Signal him to lie down when you are across the room from him, while you're talking to someone, and when there are some distractions around him. Remember to praise him enthusiastically when he goes down on the signal.

USING HAND SIGNALS

Dog owners often think of hand signals as something that only really advanced dogs can respond to, and that is partly correct. It does take some training. However, hand signals are useful for all dog owners. For example, if your dog responds to hand signals, you can give him the signal to go lie down while you're talking on the telephone, and you won't have to interrupt your conversation to do so.

Sit

If you were able to teach your Bichon to sit using the treat held above his nose, you were teaching him to sit with a hand signal. If you had to teach him by shaping him into a sit, you can still teach him a signal.

With your Bichon on his leash, hold the leash in your left hand and a treat in your right hand. Stand in front of your Bichon and take the treat from his nose upward. At the same time, whisper "Sit." When he sits, praise him and release him. Try it again. When he is watching your hand and sitting reliably, stop whispering the command and let him follow the signal. If he doesn't sit, jiggle the leash and collar to remind him that something is expected. Again, when he sits, praise him.

Stay

When you taught the stay command, you used a hand signal, the open-palmed gesture toward your Bichon's face. This signal is so obvious that your dog will probably do it without any additional training. Have your dog sit or lie down and tell him to stay using only the hand signal. Did he hold it? If he did, go back to him and praise him. If he didn't, use the leash to

To make hand signals work, your Bichon must understand that these specific movements of your hand and arm have significance. Practice verbal commands with corresponding hand gestures.

correct him (snap and release) and try it again.

Come

You want the signal for the come command to be a very broad, easily seen signal, one that your dog can recognize even if he's distracted by something. Therefore, this signal will be a wide swing of the right arm, starting with your arm held straight out to your side from the shoulder, horizontal to the ground. The motion will be to bring the hand to your chest following a wide wave, as if you were reaching out to get your dog and bring him to you.

Start teaching the signal by holding the come shaker in your right hand as you start the signal. Shake it slightly, just to get your dog's attention, and then complete the signal. Praise your dog when he responds and comes to you.

If he doesn't respond right away, start the signal again. This time, tell him verbally to come as you are making the signal and shaking the shaker. Again, praise him when he comes. Gradually eliminate the verbal command, and when your Bichon is responding well, gradually stop using the shaker.

OFF-LEASH CONTROL

One of the biggest mistakes many dog owners make is to take their dog off the leash too soon. When you take your dog

Expect and demand the same level of obedience off leash as you do on leash.

Before your Bichon is to be allowed off leash (outside of a fenced yard or your backyard), you need to make sure your Bichon's training is sound. This means he should be responding reliably and well to all of the basic commands.

Your Bichon must also be mentally mature, and in some Bichons that might be two, two-and-a-half, or even three years of age. He should be past the challenging teenage stage of development. Never take an adolescent dog off leash

off the leash, you have very little control. Only your previous training can control your dog. If you take your dog off leash before you have established enough control or before your dog is mentally mature enough to accept that control, you are setting yourself up for disaster.

Bichons are smart, curious dogs, and they love to check out new things, especially new smells. A rabbit is made to chase as far as Bichons are concerned, and so is a butterfly or bird. More than one Bichon has been so involved in his exploring that he's forgotten to pay attention to his owner's commands.

If your Bichon doesn't respond when you call him, don't repeat the command or beg him to come to you. Instead, use a long line to make him do it. Your Bichon needs to learn that come is not an optional command.

Although you shouldn't let your Bichon off leash in public places, teaching your dog to heel without a leash is a good way to avert possible hazards.

outside of a fenced-in area—that is asking for trouble.

Come on a Long Line

The long line (or leash) was introduced earlier, in the section on teaching the come command. It is also a good training technique for preparing your dog for off-leash control. Review that section and practice the come command on the long line until you are comfortable that your dog understands the come command from 20 to 30 feet away (the length of the long line) and will do it reliably.

Now take him out to play in a different place that is still safe—a schoolyard is good. Let your Bichon drag his long line behind him as he sniffs and explores. When he's distracted and not paying attention to you, call him to come. If he responds right away, praise him enthusiastically, telling him what a smart, wonderful dog he is.

If he doesn't respond right away, step on the end of the long line, pick it up, and back away from your dog, calling him again as you use the long line to *make* him come to you. Don't beg him to come to you or repeat the come command over and over. Simply use the line to make him do it. This is not an optional command!

Heel

Most places require that dogs in public be leashed. However, teaching your Bichon to heel without a leash is a good exercise. Not only is it a part of obedience competition (for people interested in that sport), but it's a good practical command, too. What would happen if your dog's leash or collar broke when you were out for a walk? Accidents happen, and if your dog has already been trained to heel off leash, disaster would be averted.

To train for this, hook two leashes up to your dog's collar.

Use your regular leash and a lightweight leash. Do a "watch me" exercise with treats, and then tell your dog to heel. Practice a variety of things—walk slowly, quickly, turn corners, and perform figure eights. When your dog is paying attention well, reach down and unhook his regular leash, tossing it to the ground in front of him. If he bounces up, assuming he's free, correct him with the second leash, "Hey! I didn't release you!" and make him sit in the heel position. Hook his regular leash back up and repeat the exercise.

When he doesn't take advantage of the regular leash being taken off, tell him to heel and start practicing the heel. Do not use the second leash for minor correction, but save it for control. If he tries to dash away, pull from you, or otherwise break the heel exercise, use that second leash and then hook his regular leash back on again.

Repeat this, going back and forth between one leash and two, until he's not even thinking about whether his regular leash is on or not. You want him to work reliably, without questioning the leash's control. For some Bichons, this may take several weeks' worth of work.

When he is working reliably, put the second leash away. Take his regular leash, hook it up to his collar, and fold it up. Tuck it under his collar between his shoulder blades so that it is lying on his back. Practice his heel work. If he makes a mistake, grab the leash and

If you admire the fluffy, well-groomed look of show dogs, you should consider using a hair dryer on your dog after his bath. Start using it when he's a pup so he will learn to enjoy the experience. Photo courtesy of Metropolitan Vacuum Cleaner Co., Inc.

bichon frise

collar as a handle and correct him. When the correction is over, take your hand off.

Expect and demand the same level of obedience off leash that you do on leash. Don't make excuses for off-leash work.

DOG SPORTS

Do you like training your Bichon? If you and your Bichon are having a good time, you may want to try one or more dog activities or sports. There are a lot of

different things you can do with your dog—some competitive, some fun, and some good works. What you decide to do depends on you and your dog.

Conformation Competition

The American Kennel Club (AKC) and the United Kennel Club (UKC) both award conformation championships to purebred dogs. The requirements vary between the registries, but basically a championship is awarded when a purebred dog competes against other dogs of his breed and wins. During competition, the judge compares each dog against a written standard of excellence for his breed and chooses the dog that most closely represents that standard.

This is a very simplistic explanation. However, if you feel your Bichon is very handsome, you might want to go watch a few local dog shows. Watch the Bichons competing and talk to some of the Bichon owners and handlers. Does your Bichon still look like a good candidate? Would you be able to keep him "in coat,"

When competing in conformation events, your Bichon will be judged on how closely he conforms to the standard for the breed.

Photo by Isabelle Francais

A well-groomed dog is a happier dog; so don't let cumbersome grooming tools stop you from getting the job done. There are compact, lightweight tools available. Photo courtesy of Wahl, USA.

grooming him as he would need to be groomed to be shown in a dog show? That grooming is a lot of work! You will also want to do some reading about your breed, about conformation competition, and perhaps even attend a conformation class.

Obedience Competition

Obedience competition is a team sport involving you and your Bichon. There are set exercises that must be performed in a certain way, and both you and your dog are judged on your ability to perform these exercises. Both the AKC and the UKC sponsor obedience competitions for all breeds of dog, as do some other organizations, including breed-specific clubs. There are also independent obedience competitions or tournaments held all over the country.

Before you begin training to compete, write to the sponsoring organization and get a copy of the rules and regulations of competition. Go to a few local dog shows and watch the obedience competitions. See who wins and who doesn't. What did they do differently? There are also a number of books on the market specifically addressing obedience competition. You may want to find a trainer in your area who specializes in competition training.

Canine Good Citizen

The Canine Good Citizen (CGC) program was instituted

AGILITY

Agility is a fast-paced sport in which the dog must complete a series of obstacles correctly in a certain period of time, with the fastest time winning. Obstacles might include tunnels, hurdles, an elevated dog walk, and more. The AKC, the UKC, and the United States Dog Agility Association all sponsor agility competitions. Bichons have done very well in agility competitions, and if you, too, are athletic, this might be a good sport for both of you.

by the AKC in an effort to promote and reward responsible dog ownership. During a CGC test, the dog and owner must complete a series of ten exercises, including sitting for petting

A good canine citizen must get along with other animals and people. This Bichon has certainly passed the test.

and grooming, walking nicely on the leash, and the basic commands sit, down, stay, and come. Upon the successful completion of all ten exercises, the dog is awarded the title "CGC." For more information about CGC tests, contact a dog trainer or dog training club in your area.

Temperament Test

The American Temperament Test Society was founded to provide breeders and trainers with a means of uniformly evaluating a dog's temperament using standardized tests. The tests may be used to evaluate potential or future breeding stock, future working dogs, or simply as a way for dog owners to see how their dog might react in any given situation. For information about temperament tests in your area, contact a local trainer or dog training club.

Flyball

Flyball is a great sport for dogs that are crazy about tennis balls. Four dogs and their owners compete against another team of four dogs. The dogs—one per team at a time—run down the course, jump four hurdles, and then trigger a mechanism that spits out a tennis ball. The dogs then catch the ball, turn, jump the four hurdles again, and return to their owners. The first team to complete the relay wins. If your Bichon likes tennis balls and is big enough to grasp one firmly in his mouth, flyball might be a fun game for the two of you. Call some local trainers or dog training clubs to see if anyone is teaching flyball in your area.

THERAPY DOGS

Dog owners have known for years that our dogs are good for us, but now researchers are agreeing that dogs are good medicine. Therapy dogs go to nursing homes, hospitals, and children's centers to provide warmth, affection, and love to the people who need it most. Bichons make great therapy dogs! For more information, contact your local dog trainer or animal shelter for information about a group in your area.

Agility is a fast-paced sport that tests your Bichon's intelligence and coordination with a series of jumps and obstacles.

Photo by Karen Taylor

bichon frise

Problem
PREVENTION
and Solving

Fortunately, Bichon Frises are not prone to many problem behaviors. They do like to jump up on people, but since they are small dogs, this is not as big a problem as it is with larger breeds. Bichons can be destructive as puppies, and this problem must be dealt with before it becomes too expensive. Bichons can also sometimes like to bark, but luckily, they rarely become problem barkers.

One of the more distressing problems that is seen in the breed is its tendency to snap or bite when overexcited, overstimulated, or startled. Some Bichons will also snap or bite to protest training or corrections, even mild ones. This can be a potentially serious behavior problem and must be addressed right away.

Although what you may consider to be problem behaviors—digging, barking, chewing—are very natural behaviors to your dog, most can be controlled or prevented.

Photo by Isabelle Francais

TRAINING

Training can play a big part in controlling problem behavior. A fair, upbeat, yet firm training program teaches your dog that you are in charge and that he is below you in the family pack. The training should also reinforce his concept of you as a kind, calm, caring leader. Your training skills also give you the ability to teach your dog what is acceptable and what is not.

Many of the behaviors that dog owners consider problems, including barking, jumping on people, chewing things, and biting or nipping, aren't problems to your Bichon. In fact, they are very natural behaviors. Dogs bark to verbalize something just as people talk. They chew when they're teething to make their gums feel better, and then they find out that chewing is fun. Dogs use their mouth (and teeth) to manipulate the world—after all, they don't have hands! All of the things you consider problem behaviors are very natural behaviors to your dog. However, most problem behavior can be addressed and either prevented, controlled or, in some cases, stopped entirely.

Photo by Isabelle Francais

Twenty percent of all commonly seen behavior problems are caused by health related problems. Make an appointment with your veterinarian if your Bichon's behavior changes.

WHAT YOU CAN DO

Health Problems

Some experts feel that 20 percent of all common behavior problems are caused by health problems. Many dogs chew on things when they're teething because their gums hurt. A bladder infection or a gastrointestinal upset commonly causes housetraining accidents. Thyroid problems can cause a behavior change, as can medications, hyperactivity, hormone imbalances, and a variety of other health problems.

If your dog's behavior changes, make an appointment with your veterinarian. Tell your vet why you are bringing the dog in, don't just ask for an exam. Explain that your Bichon has changed his behavior, describe the behavior, and ask if he could examine the dog for any physical problems that could lead to that type of behavior.

Don't automatically assume your dog is healthy. If a health problem is causing the behavior change, training or behavior modification won't make it better. Before beginning any training, talk to your veterinarian. Once health problems are ruled out, you can start addressing the problem.

Nutrition

Nutrition can play a part in causing or solving behavior problems. If your dog is eating a poor-quality food, or if he cannot digest the food he is being fed, his body may be missing some vital nutrients. If your Bichon is chewing on rocks or wood, chewing the stucco off the side of your house, or grazing on the plants in your garden, he may have a nutritional deficiency of some kind.

The use of better ingredients in your dog's food leads to better nutrition and, therefore, to better health. Make sure the dog food you choose contains only the highest quality ingredients. Photo courtesy of Nutro Products, Inc.

Photo by Isabelle Francais

Be sure to make time for play—it's a great stress reliever and is necessary for your Bichon's mental health.

Some dogs develop a type of hyperactivity when fed a high-calorie, high-fat, high-carbohydrate dog food. You may want to switch your dog to a food that has fewer calories, slightly less fat, and more meat than cereal grains. Other dogs have food allergies that may show up as behavior problems. If you have any questions about the food your dog is eating, talk to your veterinarian.

Play

Play is different from exercise, although exercise can be play. The key to play is laughter. Researchers know that laughter is wonderful medicine. When you laugh, you feel better about the world around you. Laughter and play have a special place in your relationship with your Bichon. Bichons can be very silly, and you should take advantage of that. Laugh at him and with him. Play games that will make you laugh.

Play is also a great stress reliever. Make time for play when you are having a hard time at work. Play with your Bichon after your training sessions.

Sometimes dogs get into trouble intentionally because they feel ignored. To these dogs, any attention, even corrections or yelling, is better than no attention at all. If you take time to play with your dog regularly, you can avoid some of these situations.

Prevent Problems from Happening

Because so many of the things we consider problems are natural behaviors to your Bichon, you need to prevent as many of them from happening as you reasonably can. Put the trash cans away so that he never discovers that the kitchen trash can is full of good-tasting surprises. Make sure the kids put their toys away so that your Bichon can't chew them to pieces. It's much easier to prevent a problem from happening than it is to break a bad habit later.

Part of preventing problems from occurring also requires that you limit your dog's freedom. A young puppy or untrained dog should never have unsupervised free run of the house—there is simply too much he can get into. Instead, keep him close to you and close off rooms. If you can't watch him, put him into his crate or out in the backyard.

Prevent problems before they start. Veterinarians recommend elevated feeders to help reduce stress on your dog's neck and back muscles. The raised platform also provides better digestion while reducing bloating and gas. Photo courtesy of Pet Zone Products, Ltd.

DEALING WITH SPECIFIC PROBLEMS

Biting, Nipping, and Snapping

Because these behaviors can be potentially dangerous, it is very important to make sure that your Bichon learns that snapping, biting, and nipping are not allowed, ever! Puppies use their mouth because it is natural to them. They chewed on their littermates, wrestling and play fighting. When one puppy was too rough, his brother would yelp or cry, and the biter would stop. However, that changes in a human family. Often, people allow the puppy to chew on them, making excuses like, "Oh, he's just a baby!" Worse yet, some people encourage biting by wrestling with the puppy or playing tug-of-war games with him. When the puppy learns to use his mouth on people, he will, and someday he may actually cause harm.

Teach your Bichon not to use his mouth by not allowing it to happen. Whenever he turns his mouth toward your hand or arm, even in play, use your deep voice, "No bite!" and move your hand away. If you are playing, stop the game immediately after the correction. If you

> ### EXERCISE
> Exercise is just as important for your Bichon as it is for you. Exercise works the body, uses up excess energy, relieves stress, and clears the mind. How much exercise is needed depends on your dog and your normal routine. A fast-paced walk might be enough for an older Bichon, but a young, healthy Bichon might need a good run or energetic game of fetch.

were giving him a toy or a treat when he used his mouth, take it away. Make sure he understands that using his mouth will *not* get him whatever he wants and will result in a correction and your displeasure.

If he does not react to the verbal correction, you can use your hand to close his mouth when he tries to bite. Simply close his mouth with your fingers as you tell him, "No bite!" If he protests or tries to bite again, repeat the correction. If he works himself into a temper tantrum, take him back to his crate and give him a time-out for 15 to 20 minutes. Let him out when he's calmed down.

When correcting biting, keep in mind that with some dogs, aggression begets aggression. If you show aggressive behavior toward your dog, he may respond with aggressive behavior of his own. Therefore, correct the dog enough to stop the biting, but stop the correction as soon as he gives up. Do *not* hold a grudge, do *not* rant and rave at your dog, and do *not* hit him.

Jumping on People

Just about every Bichon owner, at one time or another, has to deal with a dog that jumps up on people. That's just the way the breed is. And unfortunately, Bichons don't simply jump up—they bounce up and down as they jump. If nothing else, Bichons are enthusiastic!

Because they are small dogs, when they jump up on people, it is not as big a problem as it is with a larger dog. If you don't

You can control your Bichon's unruly behavior by having him sit or lie down.

mind that your Bichon jumps up, then simply skip this section. However, even small dogs can get muddy paw prints on your trousers, tear your pantyhose, or scratch your legs. A jumping Bichon can also be frightening to a small child.

You can control the jumping by emphasizing the sit. If your Bichon is sitting, he can't jump up. By teaching him to sit for petting, praise, treats, and his meals, you can teach him that sitting is important and that everything he wants will happen only when he sits.

Use the leash as much as you can to teach your Bichon to sit. When you come home from work, don't greet your dog until you have a leash and collar in hand. As your dog greets you, slip the leash over his head. Then you can help him sit. If he tries to jump, give him a snap and release of the leash and a verbal correction, "No jump! Sit!" Of course, as with all of your training, praise him when he sits.

When you are out in public, make sure your Bichon sits before any of your neighbors or friends pet him. Again, use the leash. If he won't sit still, don't let anyone pet him, even if you have to explain your actions, "I'm sorry, but

Photo by Isabelle Francais

If your Bichon is a problem digger, you need to concentrate first on preventing this behavior from occurring. When you cannot supervise him outdoors, put your Bichon in a dog run or crate.

I'm trying to teach him manners and he must sit before he gets any petting."

The key to correcting jumping up is to make sure that bad behavior is not rewarded. If someone pets your Bichon when he jumps up, that action has been rewarded. However, when he learns that he only gets attention when he's sitting, that will make sitting more attractive to him.

Digging

Bichons are not normally problem diggers, but they may dig an occasional hole in the garden. If your Bichon likes to dig, you need to concentrate first on preventing this problem from occurring. If you come home from work to find new holes in the lawn or garden, don't correct him then. He probably dug the holes when you first left in the morning, and a correction ten hours later won't work.

Instead, build him a dog run, put him in his crate, or otherwise restrict his freedom.

bichon frise

Then when you are home and can supervise him, you can let him have free run of the rest of your yard. When he starts to get into trouble, you can use your voice to interrupt him, "Hey! What are you doing? Get out of the garden!"

The destructive dog also needs exercise, training, and playtime every day to use up his energy, stimulate his mind, and give him time with you. Most importantly, don't let a dog that likes to dig watch you garden. If you do, he may come to you later with all of those bulbs you planted earlier.

Excessive Barking

Bichons are not normally problem barkers. However, a Bichon left alone for many hours each day may find that barking gets him attention, especially if your neighbors yell at him. Bichons also bark when they get overexcited, such as when the neighborhood kids come home from school.

Start teaching him to be quiet when you're at home with him. When your Bichon starts barking, tell him, "Quiet!" When he stops, praise him. When he understands what you want, go for a short walk outside, leaving him home. Listen, and when you hear him start barking, come

EXTRA HELP

Problem barkers may need extra help, especially if your neighbors are complaining. There are anti-bark collars on the market, and several are very humane and effective. All are triggered by the dog's barking and administer a correction to the dog. Some collars make a high-pitched sound, one squirts a whiff of citronella, and others administer a shock. I do not recommend the shock collars for Bichons, because many will panic at this correction. However, the first two collars are quite effective for many dogs.

back and correct him. After a few corrections, when he seems to understand, ask a neighbor to help you. Go outside and ask your neighbor to come out to talk. Have the kids out in the yard playing. When your dog barks because he's feeling left out, go back and correct him. Repeat as often as you need to until he understands.

You can reduce your dog's emotional need to bark if you make coming home and leaving home quiet and low-key. When you leave the house, don't give him hugs or tell him repeatedly to be a good dog—that simply makes your leaving more emotional. Instead, give him attention an hour or two prior to your leaving, and when it's time for you to go, just go. When you come home, ignore your dog for a few minutes. Then whisper hello to him. Your Bichon's hearing is very good, but to hear your whispers he is going to have to be quiet and still.

You can also distract your dog when you leave. Take a brown paper lunch bag and put a couple of treats in it—maybe a dog biscuit, a piece of carrot, and a slice of apple. Roll the top over to close it and rip a very tiny hole in the side to give your dog encouragement to get the treats. As you walk out the door or gate, hand this to your dog. He will be so busy figuring out where the treats are and how to get them, he'll forget you are leaving.

Dashing Through Doors and Gates

This is actually one of the easier behavior problems to solve. Teach your Bichon to sit at all doors and gates, then hold that sit until you give him permission to go through or get up after you have gone through. By teaching him to sit and wait for permission, you will eliminate the problem.

Start with your dog on leash. Walk him up to a door. Have him sit, tell him to stay, and then open the door in front of him. If he dashes through, use the leash to correct him (snap and release) as you give him a verbal correction, "No! Stay!" Take him back to his original position and do it again. When he will hold the sit at this door,

Your dog may be barking excessively to get attention. If your Bichon is becoming a problem barker, there are a number of techniques that will train him to be quiet.

Photo by Isabelle Francais

go to another door or gate and repeat the training procedure.

When he will wait on his leash at all doors and gates, take the leash off and hook up his long line. Fasten one end of the long line to a piece of heavy furniture. Walk him up to the door and tell him to sit and stay. Drop the long line to the ground. With your hands empty, open the door and stand aside. Because your hands are empty (meaning you aren't holding the leash), your Bichon may decide to dash. If he does, the long line will stop him, or you can step on the line. Give him a verbal correction, too, "No! I said stay!" and bring him back to where he started. Repeat the training session here and at all other doors and gates.

Photo by Isabelle Francais

It is important to teach your Bichon to sit and wait for permission before proceeding through doors and gates.

RUNNING FREE

If your Bichon does make it out through a door or gate, don't chase him. The more you chase, the better the game, as far as he's concerned. Instead, go get the shaker you used to teach the come command. Shake it and say, "Sweetie, do you want a cookie? Come!" When he comes back to you, you must praise him for coming even though you may want to wring his neck for dashing through the door. Don't correct him—a correction will make him avoid you even more the next time it happens.

Other Problems

Many behavior problems can be solved or at least controlled using similar techniques. Try to figure out why your Bichon is doing what he's doing—from his point of view, not yours. What can you do to prevent the problem from happening? What can you do to teach your dog not to do it? Remember, as with all of your training, a correction alone will not change the behavior; you must also teach your dog what he can do.

If you still have some problems, or if your dog is showing aggressive tendencies, contact a dog trainer or behaviorist for some help.

Have Some
FUN
With Your Training!

Much of training is teaching your Bichon what his place in the family is, what the household rules are, and how to control himself. That can be serious stuff. However, training can be fun, especially from a Bichon's viewpoint! Games and trick training can challenge your training skills and your Bichon's ability to learn. You can have a great time showing off your dog's tricks, amusing your friends, and just plain having fun with your dog.

Games and trick training can challenge your training skills and your Bichon's ability to learn.

DEAD DOG

I taught one of my dogs to play dead, and we both had a lot of fun with it. Michi got so good that he could pick the phrase "dead dog" out of casual conversation. One day, the son of a neighbor of mine had just graduated from the police academy and was very proud of his new uniform. Michi and I were out front, so we went over to congratulate the new police officer. As I shook the young man's hand, I turned to Michi and asked him, "Would you rather be a cop or a dead dog?" Michi dropped to the ground, went flat on his side, and closed his eyes. The only thing giving away that he really was having fun was the wagging tail! Meanwhile, my neighbor's son was stuttering and turning red. He didn't know whether to be offended or to laugh. It was great fun!

HAVE FUN WITH TRICKS

Bichons are intelligent and love to learn. When you combine this with the fact that Bichons also love to be the center of attention, you've got a dog that was just made for trick training. There's nothing a Bichon likes better than being the star of the show, so teach your Bichon some tricks and let him show off.

Shake Hands

Shaking hands is a very easy trick to teach. Have your dog sit in front of you. Reach behind one front paw, and as you say, "Shake!" tickle his leg in the hollow just behind his paw. When he lifts his paw, shake it gently and praise him. When he starts lifting his paw on his own, stop tickling.

Wave

When your dog is shaking hands reliably, tell him "Shake. Wave!" and instead of shaking

There's nothing a Bichon likes better than being the star of the show, so teach him some tricks—like waving—and let him show off.

Photo by Isabelle Francais

his paw, reach toward it without taking it. Let him touch his paw to your hand, but pull your hand away so that he's waving. Praise him. Eventually, you want him to lift his paw higher than for the shake and to move it up and down so he looks like he's waving. You can do that with the movements of your hand as he reaches for it. Praise him enthusiastically when he does it right. When he understands the wave, you can stop your hand movements.

Roll Over

With your Bichon lying down, take a treat and make a circle with your hand around his nose as you tell him, "Roll over." Use the treat in the circular motion to lead his head in the direction you want him to roll. Your other hand may have to help him. It may take some effort on your dog's part to start the roll-over movement.

Retrieving

Most Bichons like to retrieve, they just don't always understand the need to bring back what they go out after. However, once you teach your Bichon to bring back the toy, retrieving games can be great fun as well as good exercise.

Photo by Isabelle Francais

The name game is a great way to make your Bichon think. With practice, he'll learn to identify his toys by name.

If your Bichon likes to retrieve, then all you need to do is get him to bring you back the toy. When you throw the toy and he goes after it, wait until he picks it up. Once he has it in his mouth, call him back to you with a happy tone of voice. If he drops the toy, send him back to it. If he brings the toy all the way back to you, praise him enthusiastically.

Don't let him play tug-of-war with the toy. If he grabs it and doesn't want to let go, reach over the top of his muzzle and tell him "Give," as you press his top lips against his teeth. You don't have to use much pressure, just enough so that he opens his mouth to relieve the pressure. When he gives you the toy, praise him.

If your Bichon likes to take the toy and run with it, let him drag his long line behind him while he plays. Then when he dashes off, you can step on the line and stop him. Once you've stopped him, call him back to you.

The Name Game

The name game is a great way to make your dog think. And don't doubt for a minute that your Bichon can think. When you teach your Bichon the names of a variety of things around the house, you can then put him to work. Tell him to pick up your keys or your purse or send him after the remote control to the television. The ideas are unlimited.

Start with two items that are very different, perhaps a tennis ball and a magazine. Sit on the floor with your Bichon and place the two items in front of you. Ask him, "Where's the ball?" and bounce the ball so that he tries to grab it or at least pays attention to it. When he touches it, praise him and give him a treat.

When he is responding to the ball, lay it on the floor and send him after it. Praise and reward him. Now set several different items out with the magazine and ball and send him after the ball again. When he is doing well, start all over again with one of his toys. When he will get his toy, put the toy and ball out there together and send him after one or the other. Don't correct him if he makes a mistake, just take the toy away from him and try it again. Remember, he's learning a

> ### THE COME GAME FOR PUPPIES
>
> Two family members can sit on the ground or floor across the yard or down the hallway from each other. Each should have some treats for the puppy. One person calls the puppy across the yard (or down the hall), and when the puppy reaches her, she praises him and gives him a treat. She turns the puppy around so that he's facing the other family member, who then calls the puppy. This very simple game can make teaching the come command exciting for the puppy. Also, kids can play this game with the puppy, giving them a chance to participate in the puppy's training.

foreign language (yours) at the same time he's trying to figure out what the game is, so be patient.

Find It

When the dog can identify a few items by name, you can start hiding those items so that he can search for them. For example, once he knows the word "keys," you can drop your keys on the floor under an end table next to the sofa. Tell your Bichon, "Find my keys!" and help him look. Ask, "Where are they?" and move him toward the end table. When he finds them, praise him enthus–iastically.

As he gets better, make the game more challenging. Make him search in more than one room. Have the item hiding in plain sight or underneath something else. In the beginning, help him when he appears confused. But don't let him give up—make sure he succeeds.

Trick training is limited only by your imagination and your ability to teach your dog.

bichon frise

Hide and Seek

Start by having a family member pet your Bichon, offer him a treat, and then go to another room. Tell your Bichon, "Find Dad!" and let him go. If he runs right to Dad, praise him. Have different family members play the game and teach the dog each of their names so that he can search for each family member.

As he gets better at the game, the family member hiding will no longer have to pet the dog at the beginning of the game—he can simply go hide. Help your dog initially so that he can succeed at the game, but encourage him, too, to use his scenting abilities.

Touch It

Have some treats in one hand and with the other hand open wide, say "Touch my hand!" and touch your dog's nose with the palm of your hand very lightly. When his nose touches your hand, praise him (even though you did the touching) and give him a treat. Repeat several times per training session. After three or four training sessions, tell him to touch it as you hold your hand a few inches away from his nose. If he touches his nose to your palm, praise him enthusiastically.

When he is touching his nose to your palm reliably, start moving your hand to the left and right and up and down so that your dog moves around to touch it. Always praise him and give him a treat.

Now take one of the toys that your dog knows by name (from the name game) and hold it in your hand. Tell your Bichon to "Touch the toy (using the toy's name)!" You don't want him to retrieve it, just touch it. Praise him when he does it. Practice this until he is doing it well, and then repeat the exercise with different toys.

To show off, put several toys on the floor a few inches apart and tell your Bichon to touch a particular toy. Then tell him to retrieve a different toy. Go back and forth between touch and retrieve. Your friends will be astounded at how smart your dog is.

MAKE UP YOUR OWN TRICKS

What would you and your Bichon have fun doing? Teach him to stand up on his back legs and dance. Teach him to jump through a hula hoop or your arms forming a circle. Teach him to play dead, or to sneeze. Trick training is limited only by your imagination and your ability to teach your dog.